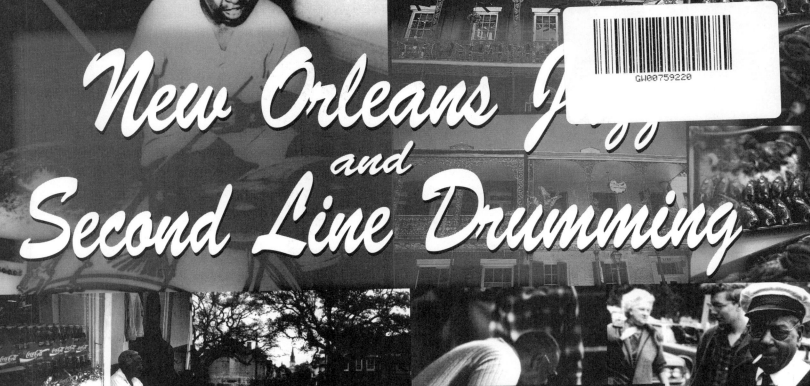

New Orleans Jazz
and
Second Line Drumming

by HERLIN RILEY and JOHNNY VIDACOVICH

Interviews by DAN THRESS

JAMES BLACK and FREDDIE KOHLMAN
Interview by VAL WILMER

Published by Manhattan Music, Inc™
© 1995 MANHATTAN MUSIC, INC.
All rights controlled and administered by Warner Bros. Publications Inc.
All rights reserved.

Acknowledgements

Special thanks to the people that made this book possible:
Paul Siegel, Rob Wallis, Dorian Romer, Emily Moorefield, Areta Buk,
Jack Waltrip, Frances Blackwell, Val Wilmer, Syndey Byrd, Charles
Suhor, Bill Huntington, Bruce Raeburn and Alma Young from the
Hogan Jazz Archives, Donald Marquis, Lary Gara and Louisiana State
University Press, Tom Stagg, Tony Scherman, Reggie Toussaint and Sea
Saint Studios, Ellis Marsalis, Wynton Marsalis, Red Tyler, Harold Battiste
and AFO Records, Jerry Brock and Barry Smith of Louisiana Music
Factory, Pete Malenverni, John Riley, Tony Martucci, Royal Hartigan,
Frank Pekoc, Bob Sherwin, Scott Fish, *Modern Drummer* Magazine, John
Norris and *Coda* Magazine, Steve Smith, Chris Parker, Adam Nussbaum,
Holly Melanson, Karen Litterer, Glenn Dicker and Scott Billington at
Rounder Records, Sally Gee of DLR/Jamb Music, Mazant Guest House,
WWOZ, Preservation Hall, New Orleans Jazz and Heritage Festival.

And a very special thanks to the musicians who participated in this project:
Herlin Riley, Johnny Vidacovich, Vernel Fournier, Smokey Johnson,
Ernie Elly, David Lee, Idris Muhammad, John Boudreaux, Earl Palmer,
Charles "Honeyboy" Otis, the Lastie family, June Gardner, David
Torkanowsky, Nicholas Payton, Chris Severen, Tony Dagradi, and
James Singleton.

*The Herlin Riley and Johnny Vidacovich material in this book is based on the
video series New Orleans Drumming, featuring Herlin Riley, Johnny Vidacovich,
Earl Palmer, and Herman Ernest. DCI Music Video, 1992. Available from
Warner Bros. Publications Inc., 1-800-628-1528 ext. 215/214.*

Production
Editor   Dan Thress
Book Design   Areta Buk
Editorial Assistant   Emily Moorefield
Music Engraving   Chelsea Music Engraving, Inc.
Cover Design   Jack Waltrip

Audio Information
Recorded November 16 and 17, 1992
by Clarence "Reggie" Toussaint
Sea Saint Recording Studio
New Orleans, LA

Mastered by Frank Pekoc
Foothill Digital
New York, NY

Produced by Dan Thress

SONG LISTING

"Oh, Didn't He Ramble"
(Will Handy)
Public Domain

"Glory, Glory Hallelujah"
(Public Domain)

"Will The Circle Be Unbroken"
(Public Domain)

"Magnolia Triangle"
(James Black)
Marzique Music/ BMI

"High Society"
(Clarence Williams, A.J. Piron)
Public Domain

"Poinciana"
(Matt Simon, Buddy Bernier, Manuel Lliso)
Hudson Bay Music/ BMI

"Carnival"
(Michael Pellera)
Pajacis Music/ BMI

"Her Mind Is Gone"
(Henry Roland Byrd)
Professor Longhair Music/ BMI

"Big Chief"
(Earl King, Wardell Quezergue)
Shirley Music/ Rated Music/ BMI

"New Orleans Cakewalk"
(Alvin "Red" Tyler)
Happy Valley Music/BMI

"New Day"
(Johnny Vidacovich)
Happy Valley Music/ BMI

"You Are My Sunshine"
(Jimmie Davis)
Peer International/ BMI

"Bongo Joe"
(James Singleton)
Urban Jym/ BMI

KEY

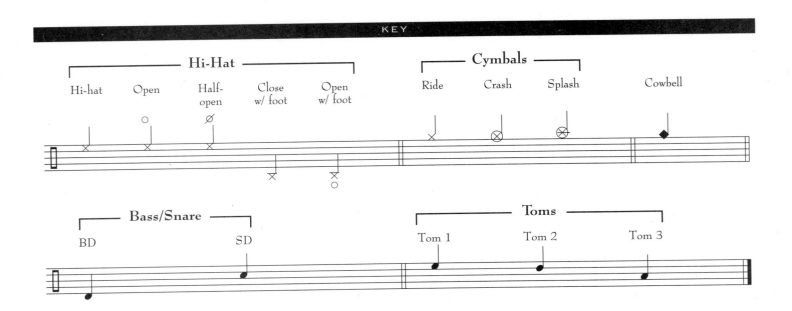

Nicholas Payton

David Torkanowsky

Tony Dagradi

James Singleton

New Orleans Drummers and Their Influence

"Black Happy" Goldston

The first drummer of great significance was Baby Dodds, the Colored veteran whose brother Johnny was such an influential pioneer among jazz clarinetists. Baby had a hand in forming the rhythmic foundation of all New Orleans jazz, both black and white, as Ray Bauduc will readily testify. In Chicago, too, Baby effected important work, personally starting Tough, Krupa and Wettling off on the right track.

After Dodds came Zutty Singleton, the same Zutty who is still today recognized as the solid man of the tubs. Less elaborate and more fundamental than Dodds, Zutty proved a beneficial inspiration and a steadying influence of both Tough and Krupa.

Tubby Hall, third among the New Orleans trap triumvirate, has always played a sober but enthusiastic type of drums which combines the light, capricious touch of Dodds with the driving, relentless power of Singleton.

—Steve Lucas
Down Beat
June 1, 1943

"Well, New Orleans has the best drummers in the world. There may be other places with other instrumentalists that do great, but the drummers were primarily from here."
—Ellis Marsalis

There is a sense of continuity to New Orleans music that comes about because its traditions are passed down within a community, by neighbors, friends and family members, rather than by anonymous strangers on a bandstand or a recording. Many New Orleans drummers know and respect their heritage, thus helping to perpetuate it; in fact, much of what is known about the evolution of New Orleans drumming comes from the musicians themselves.

The first New Orleans drummer to gain recognition outside of New Orleans was **Warren "Baby" Dodds**, a pioneer of jazz in the early 1920s. Influenced by such New Orleans drum greats as John MacMurray, Louis Cottrell Sr., Henry Zeno, Walter Brundy and Dave Perkins, Dodds incorporated the ragtime and brass band styles of the early 1900s with his own concepts as developed in the legendary bands of Fate Marable and Joe "King" Oliver. As drummer for Marable's band, Dodds performed (along with Louis Armstrong) on the riverboats which travelled from New Orleans to cities along the Mississippi. The riverboats allowed large numbers of other players to hear—and assimilate—Dodds's ideas. His move to Chicago in 1922 further increased his fame as many local drummers, including George Wettling, Dave Tough and Gene Krupa, came to study his unique style

firsthand. Dodds's playing also began to be documented on records at this time.

Among the drummers most influenced by Baby Dodds were **Zutty Singleton** and **Ray Bauduc.** Singleton and Bauduc gained national attention during the swing years of the 1940s via touring and films, and constituted a link between older forms of jazz and the new style coming out of New York called bebop.

In New Orleans, meanwhile, jazz was developing along a different path, guided in large part by two influential brothers, drummers Paul and Louis Barbarin. Born into a musical family, **Paul Barbarin** played with King Oliver, Louis Armstrong, A.J. Piron and Fats Pinchon, was the leader of his own group and was widely recorded; Louis Barbarin played with A.J. Piron, Harold Dejan, Papa Celestin, and later with bands at Preservation Hall, in a career that spanned almost seven decades. The Barbarins worked the city's parades and dance halls, creating a reservoir of traditional styles from which many up-and-coming drummers drew inspiration. Among those so inspired were Vernel Fournier and Ed Blackwell, two drummers whose work would have a lasting effect on music far beyond New Orleans. Both Fournier and Blackwell, steeped as they were in Paul Barbarin's traditional swing,

were fully able to absorb the early bop influence of Art Blakey and Max Roach.

Vernel Fournier began his career in New Orleans as a teenager in the early '40s with Dooky Chase's Young Swingsters. In 1948, while still in college, Fournier was invited to join singer King Kolax in Chicago, which eventually led to a house gig at the famous Beehive nightclub. There he worked with swing legends Lester Young, Ben Webster, Sonny Stitt, Kai Winding, and many others. Before long, Fournier was recognized as a master accompanist and brush player. His place in jazz history was secured when he joined what would become the most famous piano trio of the late '50s and early '60s, the Ahmad Jamal Trio. Fournier's contribution to Jamal's classic song "Poinciana" is a second line-jazz masterpiece.

By the early 1950s, **Ed Blackwell** had developed his trademark blend of rich New Orleans rhythm and sophisticated, Max Roach-inspired vocabulary. "That was my schooling, listening to Charlie Parker records," Blackwell said in an interview in 1992. "You know, 'Dewey Square' and all his records on Dial. I knew the owner of a drum shop, he used to order these records directly from New York for me . . . . Even before they got to New Orleans on the radio, I would get them privately." In 1951, Blackwell moved to Los Angeles, where he explored new musical territories with Ornette Coleman. After a brief return to New Orleans several years later, he moved to New York, and over the next three decades contributed to a number of important recordings by such influential artists as John Coltrane, Don Cherry, Eric Dolphy, Anthony Braxton, Booker Little, Randy Weston, Dewey Redman and Joe Lovano. Blackwell brought his dancing, second line feel to some of the world's most adventurous musical projects—and it fit perfectly.

By the time Blackwell moved to New York, he had inspired an entire generation of young drummers in New Orleans who were already adapting his ideas. This talented group included Joe "Smokey" Johnson, James Black, David Lee, Mickey Conway, John Boudreaux and Leo Morris (Idris Muhammad). Vernel Fournier's work had also impressed many up-and-coming players, the most important of which was **Earl Palmer**. Palmer began his career in New Orleans as a jazz and R&B player in the '50s, but made his mark in Los Angeles in the '60s and '70s as a session player extraordinaire. One of the most recorded drummers in history, Palmer brought the soul

Dave Bartholomew's Band at the Pelican, New Orleans. Earl Palmer, drums.

of New Orleans to the attention of the world.

Drummer **John Boudreaux**, who would later follow in Palmer's footsteps, remembered hearing Palmer play in New Orleans in the early '50s.

Cosmo [Matassa] had a small studio on Dumaine and Rampart Streets right in the French Quarter, and he had one microphone in there and that's where they would record, and every Sunday I would go watch this broadcast—Dave Bartholomew's band with Earl Palmer. It was great music, man. I mean, that was one of the few times you could hear a modern band, you know, 'cause it was mostly Dixieland and funk music, and you would very seldom hear the modern guys because people didn't pay for that kind of music. The only time you would see them was at a rehearsal at somebody's house or some club where they were rehearsing. But Dave Bartholomew was a modern kind of guy who played dance music, some funky stuff, some Afro-Cuban type stuff, and he sang and played the trumpet. Earl Palmer at that time did a couple [of songs, too] . . . but he was a phenomenal drummer. He was so smooth. He was kind of a Gene Krupa-type guy. I'm not saying he listened to Gene Krupa or he copied Gene Krupa. To me, that's the style he played [in]: very smooth and interesting, and he played good solos.[1]

Drummer and journalist **Charles Suhor** also found Palmer's playing, and its context, memorable:

The first dazzling [modern] musical influence was Earl Palmer, who played drums with bassist/singer Earl Williams's combo at the Texas Lounge near the foot of Canal Street. (I was only 15 or 16 years old, but bars were rarely checked for underage patrons in those days.) . . . Modern jazz was even further than New Orleans jazz from the vapid mainstream of postwar popular music, so the sense of inhabiting an exclusive inner circle was intensified. Only the Moldy Fig insiders knew that George Lewis was at Manny's Tavern or that there would be a Saturday afternoon jam session in the back of the New Orleans Record Shop. Only the modernist insiders knew about Ed Frank and Earl Palmer at the Texas Lounge, about Mouse Bonati and Don Suhor at Danny's Inferno in the Quarter, or about Al Belletto's combo in Biloxi . . .[2]

Earl Palmer's diverse experience with Dave Bartholomew and Earl Williams prepared him for future recording sessions with Sarah Vaughan, Count Basie, Ray Charles and Quincy Jones. Palmer, however, saw himself as an artisan rather than an innovator, as he explained to *Musician* magazine in 1992: "I'm a jazz drummer, man. People forget—us guys on those Little Richard records were playing jazz before we played rhythm and blues. There wasn't any rhythm and blues! We were just able to adapt, make things a little funky, play a shuffle instead of a jazz feel—which is how rhythm and blues, rock 'n' roll, whatever you call it, came about. People *called* it rhythm and blues. I just called it doing the job."[3]

One of the constants in the evolution of New Orleans music is the method by which information is transmitted: personally and informally, reflecting the sense of community among musicians, particularly those that play the same instrument. In addition, close ties exist between the musicians and the people of New Orleans. The result is an uncommonly open sharing of ideas and knowledge. Drummer

John Boudreaux

David Lee describes this free exchange:

Mickey Conway, John Boudreaux and me used to get [together] in Mickey's house and set up three drumsets. He had a good mother and father, they never complained. We'd do this during the summer when school was out, from about twelve o'clock in the day to about six, eight o'clock in the evening. Just trading fills, trading eights, whatever. You know, play up, play slow, play ballads, trading ideas, getting ideas from each other.[4]

Idris Muhammad also stressed the atmosphere of friendship and trust in which many New Orleans musicians developed:

It was a natural thing—John Boudreaux and Smokey and I used to practice in my house and they were the better drummers. Smokey could play all of Art Blakey's stuff, John could play all of Max Roach's things, and I was just listening. I mean, we were great friends, and I thought it was unusual that three drummers could play and be such close friends, you know, we were just trying to play the instrument.

You see, we were musical drummers. It wasn't just playing a rhythm; we used to play tunes. Playing the music of the song that we were playing, just like the horn player and the piano player, playing the changes—we were playing the music, the melody, the rhythm, the chord changes, all in one. John and Smokey used to play "Night in Tunisia" or "Nica's Dream." Smokey knew how to do this press roll that Art Blakey had. I said, "Man, how do you do it?" and he said, "Oh, you just start from here and end up heeere—bam! And that's all." John was a perfect single-stroke roller. I mean clean, man . . . . I learned a lot from these guys and they were my great friends.[5]

The music of the 1960s blurred the lines between jazz, soul and funk and created a new type of player, proficient in various musical dialects and exemplified in players such as Smokey Johnson, James Black, David Lee and Idris Muhammad. The New Orleans drummers of this era played both jazz and R&B with enough authority to produce milestones in modern jazz as well as chart-topping hit records. But, then as now, personal preference, talent, and the styles that paid best all had to be balanced in a given player's repertoire. John Boudreaux reflects on the forces that shaped his own career:

I've always wanted to play Charlie Parker's music, you know, but at the same time they were throwing all these funk gigs at us, and Dixieland gigs, so I had to learn that and I learned it, but the funk music was sort of . . . natural to me, so I fell right into that. That's not what I was pursuing, but that's what I'm known for. Most of the recording that I did was funk music.[6]

Perhaps the most memorable drummer of this generation was the late **James Black**. A multi-talented musician and composer, Black's unparalled playing remains the stuff of legend in New Orleans to this day. Drummer Ernie Elly remembers, "[Black] had the fire . . . he had the New Orleans feeling, plus different polyrhythms, cross-rhythms, everything, he was phenomenal."[7] Black moved to New York in 1961 to record with singer Tammi Lynn and stayed for six years, during which time he played and recorded with Lionel Hampton, Horace Silver, Yusef Lateef and Eric Gale before returning to New Orleans. Black died of a drug overdose in 1988 at the age of 48, but his "fire" can still be heard in his recordings and in the playing of **Herlin Riley**, a drummer who admired Black's work greatly.

Leo Morris also moved to New York in the early '60s, where he perfected his characteristic mix of New Orleans-influenced jazz, boogaloo and funk. Still an active performer and recording artist, Morris, who changed his name in the late '60s to **Idris Muhammad**, has lent his soulful grooves to recordings by James Brown, George Benson, Roberta Flack, Pharoah Sanders, Lou Donaldson, Grant Green, David "Fathead" Newman, Randy Weston, John Scofield and many others. He has influenced countless drummers including Steve Gadd, and his original rhythms, now sampled, form the basis of a wave of recent hip-hop recordings. Muhammad is, if not the best-known New Orleans drummer, certainly one of the most frequently heard.

David Lee was discovered by Dizzy Gillespie at the 1969 New Orleans Jazz and Heritage Festival, where he was playing on Bourbon street in bassist George French's band. Gillespie persuaded Lee to join his band and soon Lee was touring and/or recording with not only Gillespie, but with Joe Zawinul, Roy Ayers, Lonnie Liston Smith, Sonny Rollins, Joe Williams, Chet Baker and many others. Ernie Elly calls Lee's style "magnificent, smooth, beautiful, very melodic, very aggressive, very improvisational." Lee, whose forward thinking is evident in his compositions as well as his playing, cites Baby Dodds, Paul Barbarin and Max Roach as major influences. In New York, Lee's compelling improvisational style enhanced the work of a number of artists, notably Sonny Rollins. **Johnny Vidacovich's** melodic style, evident in his adherence to form and penchant for playing different feels within the same tune, is in many ways a continuation of Lee's work.

New Orleans has forever been a town where musical pioneers may parade down your street, be your teacher in school, or, as is

NEW ORLEANS INNOVATORS IN THE 1950s AND 1960s

"I didn't get to work with other drummers, of course, but over the years I actively sought out several from among the many wonderful players in town. They were, in roughly chronological order, Monk Hazel (when with Bonano, the ultimate swinging sideman); Freddie King (a hobbyist, in the N.O. tradition of the brilliant amateur); Earl Palmer (for me, the opener of many conceptual doors); Ed Blackwell (one of the all-time great drummers); Louis Timken (the first white drummer in town to play true bop); Reed Vaughan (in the '50s, a bopper of intense purity); Roy Burns (in town only briefly with George Gerard, he modeled great technique and taste in a Dixieland setting); James Black (who moved gracefully from Blackwell to Elvin Jones to his own style); John Boudreaux (versatile, and he walked in no one's shadow); Charlie Blancq (high-tuned, fiery bop drums in the early 60s); Jack Sperling (with Pete Fountain, a constantly joyful inventor); Nick Fatool (also with Pete, he remained fresh and inspiring); Johnny Vidacovich (a thoughtful colorist and creator in many musical contexts); Jimmy Zitano (with Al Hirt and Fred Crane, a sonic wizard).

Moving on to the musical pioneers of the 1960s, I found these artists most exciting: James Black (dr), John Boudreaux (dr), Fred Crane (p), Bill Huntington (bs), David Lee (d), Ellis Marsalis (p), Nat Perrilliat (ts), Don Suhor (as), Earl Turbinton (as), Willie (Tee) Turbinton (p, organ), and Jimmy Zitano (d). To put these musicians in context with the materials in this collection, I'll note below the clubs where I heard their music, with a Q in parentheses if the club was located in the French Quarter.

At Cosimo's (Q), James Black and Nat Perrilliat were absolutely stunning, and John Boudreaux was following a highly original path. At the Playboy and other clubs, Bill Huntington, who had switched from guitar to bass, was ever original in conception. At the Music Haven and elsewhere, Ellis Marsalis was stretching out wondrously, often with Black, Perrilliat, and Richard Payne. At the Sho' Bar, Don Suhor played incredible bebop on alto sax for strip acts. At the Black Knight Fred Crane's approaches to harmony and rhythm, with a trio that included Bill Huntington, were an intellectual and emotional tour de force. At Al Hirt's (Q), Bostonian Jimmie Zitano played unforgettable after-hours sessions with Crane, sometimes with bassists Jay Cave or Bill Huntington. At the Jazz Workshop (Q), Earl Turbinton and Willie (Tee) Turbinton and David Lee were playing state-of-the art avant garde jazz."

—Charles Suhor
Tulane University Jazz Archive, 1994

often the case, a member of your own family. This integration of music and daily life has produced some of the world's greatest musical talents, who have in turn made a lasting musical and cultural impression throughout the world.

—Dan Thress

SOURCES
1 John Boudreaux interview with Dan Thress, May 1995.
2 Charles Suhor, *Jazz in New Orleans in the 1960s.* Tulane University Jazz Archive, 1994.
3 *Earl Palmer the Rhythm Bomber, the Funk Machine from New Orleans* by Tony Scherman, *Musician* Magazine, January 1992.
4 David Lee interview with Dan Thress, New Orleans, May 1994.
5 Idris Muhammad interview with Dan Thress, New York, October 18, 1994.
6 John Boudreaux interview with Dan Thress, May 1995.
7 Ernie Elly interview with Dan Thress, New Orleans, May 1994.

"It would probably take an outsider to explain it. I guess it's just that in places like New York, they have a fast thing going. Down here it's a relaxed thing, and it's different from anywhere else—something in the way of living that's unique . . . in other words, hip, when the word is correctly used."

—Richard Payne
Bassist with the American Jazz Quintet
Down Beat, August 31, 1961

RAGTIME & BEYOND

Herlin Riley

"Well, my grandfather and I used to sit at the breakfast table eating cereal or ham and eggs, and he would grab two butter knives off of the table and just for fun, he would begin groovin' on a second line rhythm. Then he would say: "Can you do this?" And then he would just fall out laughing to see me trying to imitate and copy what he was doing. So my introduction to the early styles of New Orleans drumming was right at my kitchen table."

**EVOLUTION OF
THE "TRAPS"
1890–1920**

D.T.: *You grew up in New Orleans, so you have a lot of different influences. If we can cover some of the earlier jazz styles, the music of the jazz funerals, some of the street beats, and some of your jazz influences, maybe we can trace some of your influences.*

H.R.: All right.

Let's begin with ragtime. Can you explain a little bit about the stylistic elements of the drumming of that period?

The older musicians would say that to "rag" something is to syncopate it. For elements of surprise they would play breaks on the downbeats as well as on off-beats.

CD TRACK 2

• = staccato

RAGTIME

So a lot of the rags had syncopated rhythms in them. And in playing rag, different parts of the drumset were used for playing time. They played time on the wood block, the rim of the drum, and they also used splash cymbals. A lot of times there would be a crash cymbal, or a choke cymbal as they called it, that was usually played with a mallet. They would strike the cymbal with one hand and choke it with the other hand. And there were different techniques used for choking the cymbals. Sometimes, they would really cut off the cymbal and make it real staccato, like this:

CD TRACK 3

Or they would play other styles where they would let the cymbal ring a little bit and sustain itself, and then catch it:

CD TRACK 4

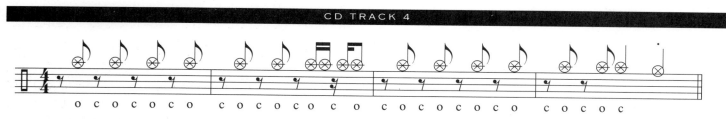

o = open
c = close with hand

So if they let it sustain, would that be used more for time playing, and the "chokes" for accents?

Well, I think it was just a matter of how they wanted to color the music at that particular spot by getting different nuances out of a certain part of the kit.

THE PRESS ROLL

What about the snare drum? What types of rolls and phrases were typical of that period?

Well, a lot of the guys used rolls on the snare drum, and if you're counting 1, 2, 3, 4, 1, 2, 3, 4, they'd play the rolls on the "and"—1 and, 2 and, 3 and, 4 and.

Is your left hand playing the "presses" and your right hand playing eighth-notes?

Yes, personally that's how I like to approach it because it helps me keep time. The right hand is pretty much keeping the pulse and the left hand is playing the press in the middle of that. So it would be something like this:

CD TRACK 5

One thing I must point out about the snare drum is that there are key elements in playing a roll that will make your roll sound cleaner. You should always play the press roll about one to one and a half inches from the edge of the rim. If you play in this area of the drum, the snare has a bit more sustain, a bit more resonance which allows the snares to rattle more, as opposed to hitting it right in the middle.

Another key to getting a good press roll is to loosen the snares on the drum. Because when you loosen the snares, the snare can vibrate more and it has more of a rattle to it.

And these were usually gut snares at the time, and smaller drums.

They were smaller wood drums, about 4 inches in depth, and the tuning lug-wing nuts, like on a bass drum, were on top. The tuning lugs tightened both the top and the bottom head at the same time.

My grandfather had a marvelous grip that would allow him to get a great press roll. Now, conventional grip is where you place the stick between your middle finger and your fourth finger, and it goes between the thumb and the index finger as well. The grip that my grandfather used was a grip where he laid the sticks across his fingers—not between his fingers—and then he covered it and balanced it with his thumb, which allowed more freedom for the stick to rebound.

When you use conventional grip and you drop the stick, you can use your fourth finger [left hand] to apply pressure to the stick and make the roll shorter. If you don't apply any pressure, then the stick can freely bounce and rebound.

Essentially you just drop it, and while holding it back behind the thumb, you pick it back up with the fingers?

Right. And that's actually how a press roll is produced. It's produced by dropping the stick [left hand], then before the stick stops vibrating or rebounding, you drop the other hand [right hand], and then before the right hand stops, you drop the left.

So we're really not thinking in terms of doubles or measured rolls, in terms of fives or anything like that.

No. Those things were part of the military style of drumming, where you play double-stroke rolls and five-stroke rolls. Military-style drumming is very even, staccato, and very rigid. But the roll that's most prevalent in New Orleans style music is the press roll.

"High Society"

In this piece, Herlin uses both "military" (measured) rolls, and press rolls. The difference is in the dynamics. He uses the measured rolls for the ensemble sections and press rolls for the softer sections.

CD TRACK 6

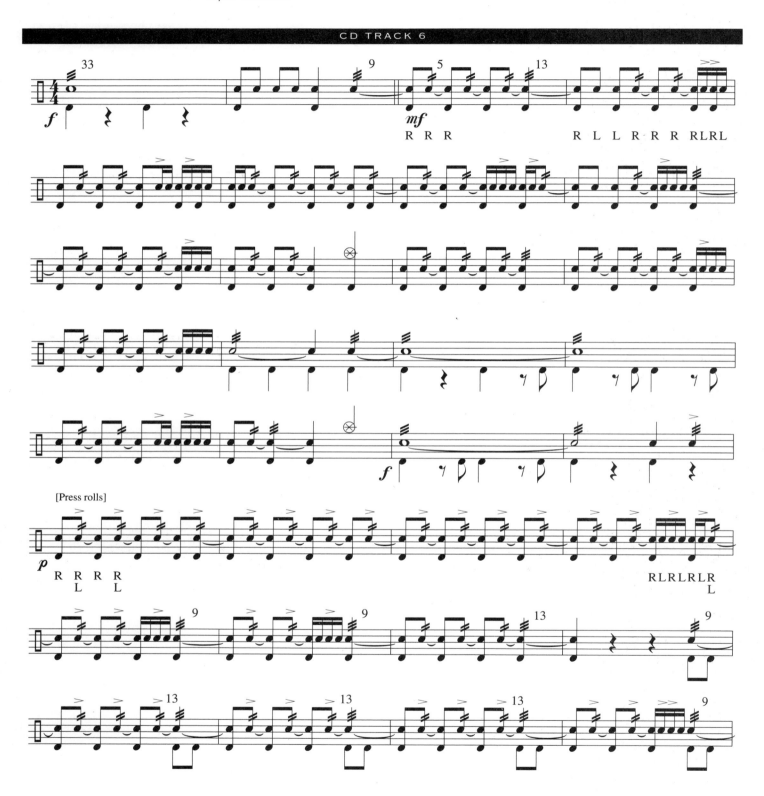

BRASS BANDS

Did the military bands of the late 1800s influence any of the early jazz styles?

Yes, like some of the early sousa marches. If you listen to the early New Orleans brass bands, they played a lot of marches but they played them with a lilt. And the lilt came from the bass drum. For instance, an ordinary march may sound like this:

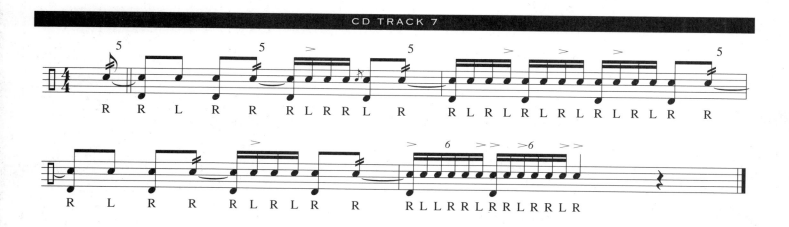

THE BASS DRUM

Now a New Orleans brass band, what they did with that was they played the bass drum on the "and" of beat 4, which gave the music a "hump." It's like a little push, so the bass drum went:

Now we'll put it all together. Check it out:

That's great, putting the syncopation in there.

Yes. And that one simple thing was the beginning of the evolution to jazz. The first jazz bands were brass bands. That was a very significant part of the style of that music. And still is, as a matter of fact, to this day. You know, that's what's most significant about drummers who come from New Orleans is the different patterns that they play on the bass drum, and how the bass drum is applied to the music.

Here are some more bass drum patterns that are pretty typical of New Orleans music:

"The bass drum is very important in the style of drumming that we play here in New Orleans, because the first thing you hear in the parades is the bass drum. You know when you hear that beat from far away, 'Man, it's a parade!' Our bass drum was the main thing. In Dixieland jazz, the bass drum was the thing. The bass drum and the snare drum—they were both important, but the bass drum most of all."

—James Black
Modern Drummer
December, 1982

Paul Barbarin

"AND" OF 4

Yeah, it's starting to get pretty funky.

Yeah! And if you notice, the one thing that's common in all those patterns that I played was the accent on the "and" of 4. And everything in the music kind of leads to that.

Now it's also important to mention that these parts are usually played by a bass drummer—

Yes, there would be a drummer who had a bass drum on a harness for marching, and he also has a cymbal attached on top to the hoop on the left side. And they would use a beater, it would be like a wire circle—

Like for a hatband.

Yes, and there would be a wooden handle on the bottom that he could hold it [usually with his left hand]. And he would strike it with the metal part, the wire hatband-looking part.

And the rhythm played on the cymbal would be afterbeats.

Yes. And he would play the drum with a different mallet in his right hand.

BASS DRUM & CYMBAL

Can you demonstrate one of those bass drum patterns with your hi-hat playing the afterbeat cymbal pattern?

OK.

CD TRACK 11

All right. Now how about the snare drum part?

Oh, you wanna add that? All right.

CD TRACK 12

From two players down to one—that essentially is the beginning of the evolution of the drumset.

Yes, that's exactly right. The guys started playing the drumset in cafes, honky-tonks, speakeasies and so forth, accompanying piano players during the ragtime era. Most of the drummers were doubling; they played in New Orleans street bands and in the cabarets and so forth with the piano players. Most of the musicians during this time were also craftsmen, some were barbers, bricklayers, painters, and so on.

TRAPS

So what would be some of the typical patterns that would be played?

OK, a lot of times there would be typical march patterns that they would play on the wood block—

CD TRACK 13

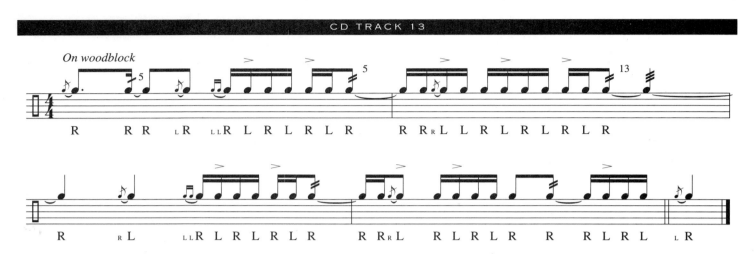

They would also play on the rim of the drums and back then, the rims or hoops were wood. So that produced a different kind of sound, it was a little softer than the wood block. I'll give you an example on these metal rims:

CD TRACK 14

They would also sometimes play on the shell, on the top of the bass drum.

CD TRACK 15

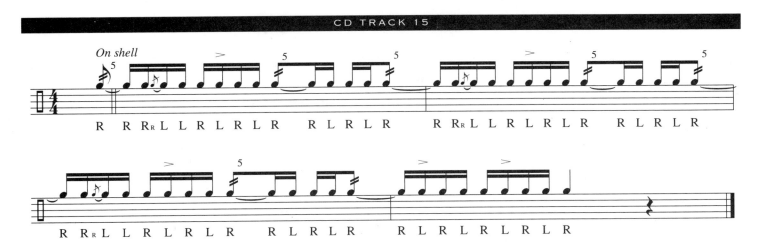

Now, all these sound very similar in timbre, but in the music there are changes that take place and sometimes they're very subtle. You don't know exactly what it is, but you know that there was some change that took place, and drummers would use these subtleties to enhance the music.

If drummers wanted to play louder than what the instruments could produce, then they would play with the back of the stick, which would be a bit louder. I'll give you an example on the wood block. Here it is with the keen part [tip] of the stick:

CD TRACK 16

Now the back part of the stick:

CD TRACK 17

There's a significant difference in volume there.

You made the most of what you had, and played different parts of the kit, the "traps," for different parts of the tune?

Yes.

"Oh, Didn't He Ramble"

The traditional tune, "Oh, Didn't He Ramble" provides a perfect vehicle for demonstrating the different color changes and nuances of traditional drumming. Herlin kicks off the tune with a street beat cadence for trumpeter Nicholas Payton. When the solos come around, Herlin accompanies pianist David Torkanowsky on the washboard; Payton, now with a mute, on the woodblock; and bassist Chris Severen with the rim of the snare drum. The timbre and dynamic level gradually decreases for each instrument. The solos are rounded out with Herlin taking a snare drum solo punctuated by woodblock, cowbell and cymbal chokes. This is a great solo that demonstrates how much you can get out of the kit without the use of the hi-hat and toms.

CD TRACK 18

Biff Shots and Shimmy Beats

I was struck with the range and constant shifting of tonal colors Baby Dodds displayed as he moved all over his set, and as he continued to vary the sound of his beat according to soloist, development of solo, and other changing contextual needs within a single piece.

—Max Roach
The Jazz Makers
Modern Drummer, 1984

"It was my job to study each musician and give a different background for each instrument. When a man is playing, it's up to the drummer to give him something to make him feel the music and make him work. That's the drummer's job. Those words were told to me by my teacher, [Walter] Brundy, when I first started to drum. The drummer should give the music expression, shading, and the right accompaniment. It's not just to beat and make a noise. I played differently for each instrument in the band."

—Warren "Baby" Dodds

Warren Dodds was born on Christmas Eve 1894 into a musical family. His grandfather had drummed in Congo Square; his older brother Johnny, who had played clarinet from an early age, was Warren's first musical role model. "Baby," as he would soon be known, drew freely on the experience of New Orleans drumming pioneers such as John MacMurray, who played parades with the John Robichaux band. "He played beautiful drums," Dodds recalled years later. "When he made a roll, it sounded like he was tearing paper." Another who impressed the young Dodds was legendary drummer and teacher Louis Cottrell, who played both parade and dance music. Dave Perkins taught Dodds the rudiments, and Walter Brundy, who also worked with John Robichaux, trained him in the fundamentals of reading music. Henry Zeno, Henry Martin and Tubby Hall all passed along pointers and information. Buddy Bolden was an ongoing source of inspiration whom Dodds often saw perform in Lincoln Park. In addition to street parade jazz, Dodds absorbed the sounds of the "piano professors," Jelly Roll Morton and Tony Jackson.

By the age of 16, Baby Dodds had sat in with various groups and was working full-time with Willie Hightower's band, the American Stars. The American Stars played a mixture of classics and swing tunes and worked mostly outdoor gigs, such as lawn parties and fish fries. An offshoot of this band, formed when trombonist Roy Palmer landed a job at the Fewclothes Cabaret in New Orleans's tenderloin district, featured Baby on drums and Sidney Desvigne on trumpet. Roy Palmer's group played a wide range of styles including syncopation (later called ragtime), and a slower, Spanish-inflected type of blues, as well as creole-influenced mazurkas, quadrilles, schottisches and polkas, all popular dances of the day.

After the American Stars, Dodds joined Frankie Duson's Eagle Band, which included trumpeter Bunk Johnson. With Dodds on snare drum, the Eagle Band played social club-sponsored street parades as well as funerals. But it was in his next band that Dodds started to come into his own as a drummer. As drummer for Sonny Celestin's group,[1] he developed his infamous "shimmy" beat, inspired by the moves of a French soldier Dodds had once seen dancing. He described the shimmy as "a contrast of moving your shoulders and stomach while drumming, and not missing a beat." The shimmy beat remained a Baby Dodds trademark throughout his career.

In 1918, Dodds joined the Fate Marable Band and worked for the next three years on the Mississippi riverboats, along with a young trumpeter named Louis Armstrong. The riverboats worked mostly in St. Louis in the summer months, occasionally going as far north as St. Paul, with stops in Iowa, Wisconsin and Minnesota, and returning to New Orleans for the winter. The music on the riverboats was strictly standards and dance tunes, with the blues played only in New Orleans. Nevertheless, the Marable Band had a high level of musicianship, and with them Dodds perfected his time playing and comping style.

It was on the riverboat that I began using the rim instead of the woodblocks. I don't remember the [name of] the number, but on one that called for woodblocks, I used the rim of the bass drum instead. And it sounded so pretty. The woodblock gave a loud sound, and I substituted the shell of the drums and it sounded so soothing and soft. Sometimes I used faster beats on the rims. Then again, when it was a slow number, I'd do it in triplets. It was pretty and soft, and still it would make the number lively. I worked out these things by myself on the boat because I knew I had to make good. That's also where I learned to be so tough on drumming. At that time I could sit down and drum a pretty long time.

In 1921, both Dodds and Armstrong left the riverboats. When word reached cornetist and bandleader Joe Oliver that Baby Dodds was available, he invited both Baby and Johnny, Dodds's clarinetist brother, to join Oliver's band in San Francisco. The brothers promptly left for the coast, where they played dances in cities such as Fresno, San Jose and Santa Cruz for a year. In 1922 the band moved to Chicago, where Louis Armstrong joined them, and they began an engagement at Lincoln Gardens.

Joe Oliver's group was a dance band steeped in New Orleans tradition and the perfect situation for Dodds:

Joe Oliver's band was the sort of group where you could use your own experiences and eventually get a chance to work them out with the outfit. I used woodblocks on my part in "Dippermouth," but on most numbers I used the shells or rims of the drums instead. I did very little on the woodblocks and much more on the shells. They weren't as sharp. The woodblock gave a tone that was too shrill and sharp for the band. The sound of the rim was much better. It was up to me to bring out the different expressions for the outfit. If I would be drumming straight and felt that a roll would bring out an expression, I used that. Or if I were playing along and felt that beating the cymbal would help the number, I would do that. It was up to all of us to improve the band in its jazz, and I had to do my part."

The original Oliver band had broken up by 1925, and several of its members, including

The photos at left, dating from the 1940s, illustrate Dodds's setup. Note the different cowbell sizes, the location of the woodblock and the placement of the two cymbals. In the bottom frame Dodds has his sticks on the wooden hoop of the bass drum. With his two smaller cowbells positioned towards him, this would leave a small playing area that he refers to as the shell or "rim" of the bass drum.

BABY DODDS SELECTED DISCOGRAPHY

Louis Armstrong *The Hot Fives and Hot Sevens, Vol. 2, The Hot Fives and Hot Sevens, Vol. 3* (Columbia), *Louis Armstrong of New Orleans* (MCA/Decca); **Sidney Bechet** *The Victor Sessions, Master Takes 1932–43* (Bluebird); **Johnny Dodds** *Blue Clarinet Stomp* (Bluebird), *South-Side Chicago Jazz* (MCA/Decca); **Bunk Johnson** *The King Of The Blues, Bunk Johnson 1944* (American Music); **George Lewis with Kid Shots** (American Music); **Jelly Roll Morton** *The Centennial Jelly Roll Morton: His Complete Victor Recordings* (Bluebird)

Baby and Johnny Dodds, were hired by banjo player and club owner Burt Kelly to play at Burt Kelly's Stables. This and other gigs kept Baby Dodds in Chicago until 1936, years that were crucial to the development of jazz. The influence of Baby Dodds on drummers and bandleaders in Chicago is a key element in an entire lineage of drummers not usually associated with New Orleans music.

A lot of the fellows who later hit the big money in the swing era learned from us oldtimers. And much of [the information] was obtained at these Chicago sessions . . . . A lot of drummers picked up different things from my playing. George Wettling often watched me at Lincoln Gardens and he once asked me to show him how I held my drumsticks when I worked. I showed him and for a while his drumming was very much like mine. Dave Tough used to come to listen to us at Burt Kelly's Stables and the K-Nine Club. He watched me closely, but of course, he had been drumming ever since high school and he was already a very good drummer.

I knew Ray Bauduc from the old days in New Orleans, but he used to come to watch and listen when we were playing at the Three Deuces. Bauduc liked my drumming and he used to ask me how to do various things. Gene Krupa came around for some pointers, too. Long before that, Gene came to Kelly's Stables and I showed him how I tuned my drums and what size drumsticks I used. A lot of white musicians got ideas and pointers from me but I never really taught anyone how to drum.

I was the inspiration of another fellow who became a very famous drummer, Zutty Singleton. His uncle, Willie Bontemps, used to love my drumming. He once asked his uncle, "I wonder, Will I ever drum like that fellow?" I never taught Zutty a thing but I was his inspiration.

Dodds recorded with numerous groups in Chicago, including two which were not performing bands but early studio projects, Louis Armstrong's Hot Seven and Jelly Roll Morton's Red Hot Peppers. He also worked with bandleader Sidney Bechet, and for his brother, Johnny Dodds. In 1944, Baby Dodds moved to New York and recorded with the Bunk Johnson Band for Bill Russell's American Music label, as well as for Decca and RCA Victor the following year. In 1947 he appeared on a radio program entitled *This is Jazz,* which featured a mix of New Orleans and New York musicians in a performance that was one of the highlights of his career. In 1946 he recorded a series of interviews and drum solos for an album entitled *Baby Dodds, Talking and Drum Solos* (Folkways Records). On this disc, Dodds demonstrates his drum parts to several standard tunes and improvises a few pieces, including "Tom-Tom Workout" and "Nervebeats," as well as playing and explaining his press roll. The listener can't help but be impressed with how "modern" this early pioneer sounded on the drums.

After several years in New York, Dodds made his first trip to Europe in 1948, on tour with Mezz Mezzrow's band. In France, he met many musicians who had learned from records to play in the styles to which he had contributed so significantly. The French musicians embraced Dodds and other jazz musicians, who were in turn grateful for the recognition, respect and first-class treatment they so rarely experienced at home.

Dodds played a year-long engagement at the Beehive in Chicago in 1948. In April of 1949, after returning to New York, he suffered a stroke and went back to Chicago where he recuperated, only to suffer a second stroke in 1950. Although he did play on a few more occasions and gave musical advice to several groups, Baby Dodds's long and influential playing career was at its end. He died on February 14, 1959.

SOURCES
The Baby Dodds Story, As Told to Larry Gara, Revised Edition, 1992, Louisiana State University Press
Baby Dodds, Talking and Drum Solos, Liner Notes edited by Frederic Ramsey, Jr. Folkways Records, 1951

QUOTES
All quoted material is from *The Baby Dodds Story.*

NOTES
1 The other members of Celestin's group at this time were: Bebé Ridgely, trombone; Willie Bontemps (uncle of Zutty Singleton), bass and guitar; Lorenzo Tio, clarinet; Sonny Celestin, trumpet.

PAUL BARBARIN

ARTHUR "ZUTTY" SINGLETON

PAUL BARBARIN
SELECTED DISCOGRAPHY

Henry "Red" Allen *Henry "Red" Allen And His New York Orchestra 1929–1930* (JSP), *Henry "Red" Allen And His New York Orchestra 1929–1930 Vol. 2* (JSP), *Henry "Red" Allen 1933–1935* (Classics), *Henry "Red" Allen 1936–1937* (Classics), *Henry "Red" Allen 1937–1941* (Classics); **Louis Armstrong** *Louis Armstrong 1923–1931* (BBC), *Louis In New York Vol. V* (Columbia), *Louis Armstrong & His Orchestra 1934–36* (Classics), *Louis Armstrong & His Orchestra 1937–38* (Classics), *Louis Armstrong & His Orchestra 1934–36* (Classics); **Paul Barbarin as a leader** *Streets Of The City, Paul Barbarin And His Band* (Storyville), *Paul Barbarin And His New Orleans Jazz* (Atlantic); **Johnny Dodds** *Johnny Dodds, 1926–1940: Part One* (Affinity); **George Lewis** *Jazz In The Classic New Orleans Tradition* (Original Jazz Classics); **Jelly Roll Morton** *The Complete Jelly Roll Morton 1926–1930* (RCA Bluebird), *Jelly Roll Morton Volume Two* (JSP), *Jelly Roll Morton 1928–1929* (Classics); **Joe "King" Oliver** *King Oliver Volume One 1923 To 1929* (BBC), *King Oliver Volume Two 1927 To 1930* (BBC), *1926–1931 Complete Vocalion/Brunswick Recordings* (Affinity); **Luis Russell** *Savoy Shout* (JSP); **Louis Barbarin; Percy Humphrey** *A Portrait Of Percy Humphrey* (Storyville); **Compilation** *The 77 Session* (GHB)

ARTHUR "ZUTTY" SINGLETON
SELECTED DISCOGRAPHY

Henry "Red" Allen *Henry "Red" Allen 1937–1941* (Classics); **Louis Armstrong** *Louis Armstrong 1923–1931* (BBC), *Louis Armstrong And Earl Hines Vol. IV* (Columbia), *Hot Fives And Sevens Vol. 3* (JSP), *Louis Armstrong, Volume 1V, Armstrong And Earl Hines* (Columbia Jazz Masterpieces); **Sidney Bechet** *The Chronological Sidney Bechet, 1937–1938* (Classics), *Sidney Bechet, 1932–43: The Bluebird Sessions* (BMG/Bluebird); **Roy Eldridge** *Roy Eldridge Little Jazz* (Columbia Jazz Masterpieces); **Lionel Hampton** *Lionel Hampton 1929 To 1940* (BBC), *Lionel Hampton 1939 To 1940* (Classics); **Jelly Roll Morton** *The Complete Jelly Roll Morton 1926–1930* (RCA Bluebird), *Jelly Roll Morton Volume Two* (JSP), *The Jelly Roll Morton Centennial—His Complete Victor Recordings* (RCA), *Jelly Roll Morton: New Orleans Memories & Last Band Dates* (Commodore, released by Atlantic); **Kid Ory** *New Orleans Legends* (Vogue); **Charlie Parker** *The Genius Of Charlie Parker* (Savoy); **Pee Wee Russell** *Jack Teagarden/Pee Wee Russell* (Original Jazz Classics), *Pee Wee Russell Trio 1941* (Commodore); **Thomas "Fats" Waller** *Jazz Classics: Fats Waller 1927–1934* (BBC), *The Joint Is Jumpin'* (RCA Bluebird), *The Last Years 1940–1943* (RCA Bluebird), *Fats Waller And His Rhythms—The Last Years (1940–1943)* (RCA Bluebird) [Three Deuces and Hot Four (Commodore)]; **On film:** *Stormy Weather* (1943), *New Orleans* (with Louis Armstrong) (1946), *Turned Up Toes* (1949)

Paul Barbarin

Arthur "Zutty" Singleton

THE WASHBOARD

What about the washboard, I see you have a washboard behind your drums.

Well, the washboard was typical pretty much in what they would call "spasm bands." Now, spasm bands were bands that played around New Orleans, and they made musical instruments out of stuff they found around the house.

One of the instruments that has remained from this era is the washboard. Most of the cajun or zydeco bands around Louisiana still use the "wash plate" [or "rubboard"] as part of the rhythm section.

So show us some of those techniques. And what are you using for a beater?

Well, right now I'm going to use a triangle beater, but most times, they put thimbles on their fingers or on the ends of gloves. To give you an example, here are some New Orleans rhythms that you can play on the washboard.

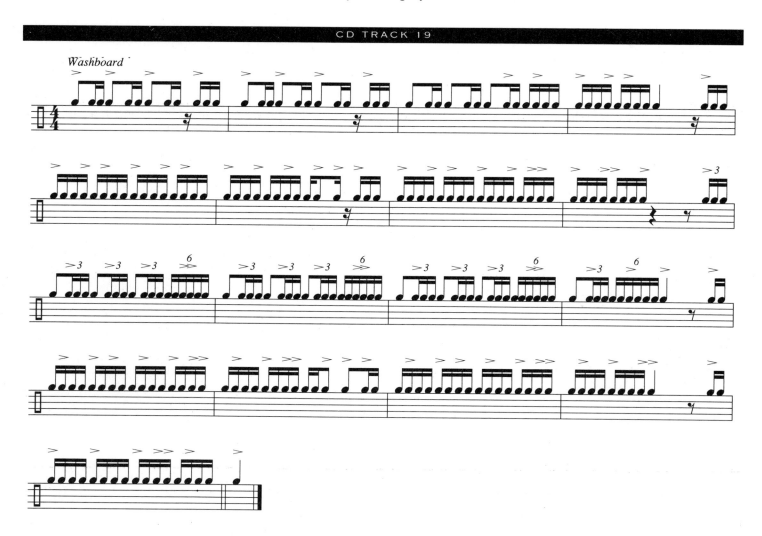

I was reading this book on Baby Dodds and it said that when Baby was playing on the riverboats going up and down the Mississippi one of the guys from Ludwig, I think it was William F. Ludwig, noticed that Baby always tapped his left foot while he played. So he came in one day and measured Baby's foot. And then he came back a week or two later with a sock cymbal, which at the time was called a "lowboy."

Lowboy, because it was low to the ground.

Yeah, it was a short version of a sock cymbal. And Baby played it a couple of times, but he didn't really like it. Then in the 1930s it really came into play, and by then it had been raised up to where it pretty much is today.

So you could play it with your sticks.

Right. And I guess the drummer who was most significant for his work with the hi-hat at that time would be Papa Jo Jones. When Papa Jo Jones started playing on the hi-hat, that pretty much took the basic pulse in jazz from the bass drum and brought it to the top of the kit. So it went from the lowest timbre of the kit to the highest timbre of the kit—the cymbals.

BRUSHES

JOE "KING" OLIVER

What about the origin of brushes?

I think what happened was, during the rag era, when drummers started playing indoors, it became necessary to play softer. I think [trumpeter/bandleader] King Oliver and Baby Dodds had a lot to do with the idea of using brushes. King Oliver played with mutes all the time—he was a master of mute playing—and when Baby worked with him, I think he might have suggested, "Why don't you play a little softer, man?" So somebody came up with some flyswatters, and Baby checked them out, played them for a while, he said, "Yeah, OK." And there's also a story that the earlier brushes were whisk brooms that people used to dust off their clothes. Brushes really found their place around the '30s, along with the hi-hat.

Do you know what the early techniques were? Were they essentially the same in terms of the left hand moving around the head and the right hand playing a time figure?

I think that was pretty much it and they also used what I call the windshield-wiper technique in which the left hand goes back and forth on quarters and the right hand plays the basic swing pattern:

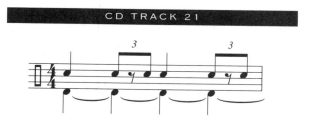

CD TRACK 21

That pattern has pretty much been around since then.

DEACON LASTIE

Let's talk again about your grandfather, Frank Lastie. He was a church Deacon here in New Orleans, and he was the first drummer to bring the drums into church, which was around 1927. Can you go over some of the things he showed you as far as the rhythms he was playing in church?

Well, my grandfather and I used to sit at the breakfast table eating cereal or ham and eggs, and he would grab two butter knives off of the table and just for fun, he would say: "Can you do this?"

CD TRACK 22

Deacon Frank Lastie

And then he would just fall out laughing to see me trying to imitate and copy what he was doing. So my introduction to the early styles of New Orleans drumming was right at my kitchen table.

He would also play that kind of beat or groove in church. And there was also another groove he always played in church which sounded like this:

CD TRACK 23

etc.

TIME

So in checking him out, I began to realize the significance of how the music was supposed to feel. Early on, he always stressed to me, "Man, when you learn how to play, learn how to play time." Because when I first started to play the drums, I wanted to play all kind of wild stuff all over the drums. I'd get in church and I'd go into all this wild stuff and he'd look at me and give me the eye: "Hey man, what are you doing back there?" And I knew right away to go back into playing time. He often stressed to me that time was the most important function of the drummer.

There's a way of playing time that's organic, and there's a way of playing time that's really not. To me, you're playing time organically when you're playing a groove. And to me, a groove starts off perhaps with a beat, but then the groove grows. You can play a phrase where you kind of play a little bit behind the beat, you can play a phrase where it's a little bit above the beat. There are different ways to manipulate the beat that you start off with. And when you manipulate it in that way that feels good to everybody you're playing with—and I don't mean playing randomly for the sake of doing it—I mean when the music dictates it to you, that "Hey, you can leave this out next time, or you can put a fill here or put a fill there," to me, that's organic and that's when the music is grooving.

David, Betty Ann, and Walter Lastie

Your mother's a gospel singer and she was gracious enough to come in and play with you today. Can you describe what you're going to play?

We're going to do two tunes. One is called "Will the Circle Be Unbroken," and the other is called "Glory, Glory Hallelujah." What I'd like to say about these two tunes and the feeling of what we're going to play, is that this is pretty much what went on in our house. We always got together on holidays or any given weekend or day, and we played music.

There was a piano, and my grandfather had some drums there, and I had a couple of other uncles who played sax and trumpet [trumpeter Melvin Lastie and saxophonist David Lastie toured and recorded with numerous R&B bandleaders throughout the '50s and '60s] and they would come together and we'd all usually jam on gospel tunes.

Betty Ann Lastie Williams

Gospel

"Glory, Glory Hallelujah"

CD TRACK 24

DRUMS

"Will The Circle Be Unbroken"

CD TRACK 25

DRUMS

WALTER "POPEE" LASTIE

Your playing is so musical, you can hear melodies and the song form so well.

Well that was something I got from my uncle "Popee"—Walter Lastie. [Walter Lastie also studied drums in church under the watchful eye of his father, Deacon Frank Lastie]. Whenever he would sit down and tell me anything about playing the drums, he would always say, "Whenever you play a solo, think of the melody and try to play the form of the tune so that people can relate to it." As opposed to just playing just a beat or playing a lot of wild licks. Whatever I play, I always try to make it musically coherent.

Can you show me that slick move you played during your solo with your stick on the bass drum head?

Man, that's a direct quote from my grandfather, Frank Lastie. Whenever he'd feel good he'd reach down and do something like this: [Herlin demonstrates "backhanding" his right stick against his bass drum head while playing a 3-note pattern between his right foot, left hand and right hand on the bass drum]

That was before the double bass drum pedal came in!

That's right, who needs it!

'HE WHO SINGS PRAYS TWICE'

A TRIBUTE TO POPEE AND THE LASTIE FAMILY

A NIGHT TO REMEMBER

AFTER THE SUPERBOWL AT TIPITINA'S JAN.25 501 NAPOLEON AVE

WALTER DANIEL LASTIE ★ SEPT.18,1938 - DEC.28,1980

A MUSICAL BENEFIT IN RESPECT FOR THE FAMILY. APPEARING: Deacon Frank Lastie ★ David Lastie ★ Betty Anne Lastie Williams ★ Herlin Riley ★ Jos. Lastie,Jr ★ Richard Knox ★ Tommy Ridgeley ★ Mike Vice ★ Eddie & Toni Bo ★ Al "Carnival Time" Johnson ★ Jessi "Naturally" Hill ★ Oliver "Who Shot the La La" Morgan ★ Johnny Adams ★ Reggie Hall ★ Walter Washington ★ Zigaboo Modeliste ★ Scotty Hill ★ Otis Bazoon ★ George Porter an Joyride ★ Dave "Fat Man" Williams ★ Irma Thomas and the Professionals(special ½ hr appearance) ★ Rickie Castrillo ★ Dr.Frank Minyard ★ Aaron Neville ★ Spencer Bohren ★ David Torkanowski ● ● ● friends, musicians, and R & B music lovers. Beginning at 8PM with a special showing of Up From The Cradle of Jazz "A Profile of the Lastie Family (part 1 of a documentary on New Orleans Music Families) ★ The Restaurant will be open $3.00 donation gratefully accepted at the door. Children free. Music from 9PM ● ● ●

JAZZ FUNERALS

Can you explain a little about the tradition of the jazz funerals, beginning with the dirge, and the role of the drummer.

I think the dirge goes back to the old brass bands, which came from the old military bands of the Civil War. There's a funeral march they used to play in military bands that sounded a lot like a dirge. And that beat went like this:

Eureka Brass Band with Robert "Son Fewclothes" Lewis on bass drum.

SECOND LINE

A New Orleans dirge is pretty much the same beat, and they just play hymns over that, so you'd have something like—

"A Closer Walk with Thee"

"A Closer Walk with Thee" or "In the Sweet By and By"—

And these would be played in the street going from the church to the gravesite.

Yes, to the gravesite. And years ago, people marched very slowly and solemnly behind the deceased. And they would play that slow and solemn kind of beat, and there would be hymns that were played on top of the beat. And after you "planted" the body in the cemetery, there would be what they would call "cut the body loose" which means that, on the way back from the cemetery, they would strike up an upbeat kind of song like "Oh, Didn't He Ramble," or "Just A Little While to Stay Here." So you might hear a trumpet player play the first few bars of an uptempo tune, while the drummers are playing some sort of cadence. Then the trumpet player gives the cue; do-dit, do-dit. At the cue, the drummers would play a roll off going into the start of the tune. That means we're going to the "up" part of the procession. So I'll give you a little bit of that:

CD TRACK 28

So the rhythm that you play coming back from the cemetery became known as "second line."

Yes, the term second line came from the mourners and the revelers, because the body would be in front along with the close relatives, people who were mourning the deceased. Everybody else would be behind, in the second line.

Second line, parade beats and street beats—similar terminology for the same thing.

Yes, just similar terminology for the same thing.

Let's talk about Vernel Fournier and the groove he played on "Poinciana." You've worked with Ahmad Jamal and you've recorded three albums with him, and I'm sure you played that tune in concert. Can you show us what you played?

Well, it's directly from the New Orleans-style parade beats.
[Herlin picks up a pair of mallets and turns his snares off]

"Poinciana"

DRUMS

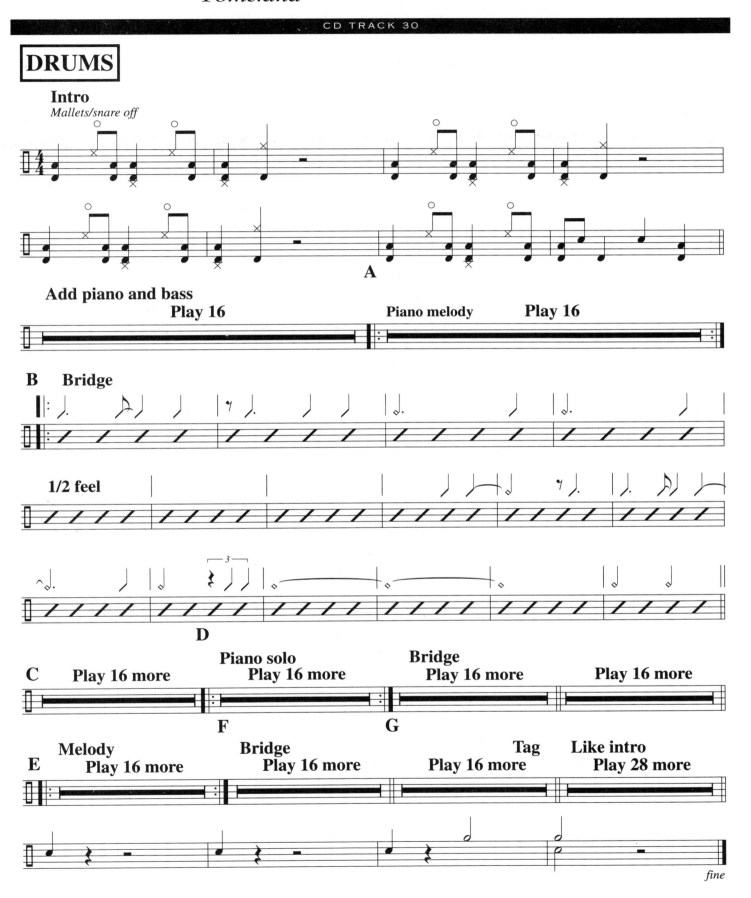

VERNEL FOURNIER

Dancing in the Sixth Ward

"I got out of the service December 10, 1945, and the following week I went to a concert where Billy Eckstine's band was playing and the local band that played before them was Dooky Chase. Vernel Fournier was playing drums in Dooky's band and Art Blakey was with Billy Eckstine's band. I heard both those drummers that night and said, "That's it. I'm going to play drums."

—Earl Palmer
Modern Drummer
May, 1983

I was born in what they call Treme (tra-may), the heart of New Orleans. The sixth ward. Rampart Street to Broad St., Canal to Esplanade. That's where all the dancers were. San Jacinto Hall, Economy Hall, the Coliseum, the Gypsy Tea Room, these were the major clubs. To go dancing, you had to come to the sixth ward.

—Vernel Fournier

Vernel (one "L") Fournier (Forn-yea) has been a resident of New York by way of Chicago since 1979. His journey is typical of other New Orleans drumming legends who migrated north and had a big impact on the larger musical community. Beginning in New Orleans, Vernel's story captures the soul of the early New Orleans drumming experience: the influence of the legendary Paul Barbarin, the development of bop drumming, the swinging Chicago scene and his days with Ahmad Jamal. Vernel's contribution to Jamal's arrangement of "Poinciana" is a drumming landmark. His sophisticated touch with brushes and funky, timely comping with the bass drum has inspired us for decades, and the sophisticated and cool arrangements of the Jamal trio have influenced musicians from Miles Davis to Keith Jarrett. Vernel's drumming is on the same masterful level as that of Art Blakey, Kenny Clark, Max Roach and "Philly" Joe Jones, drummers who have changed and expanded the language of the instrument.

You were born July 30th, 1928?
That's right.

Are you from a musical family?
No. I had an uncle, Emile Bagneris, whose nickname was "Al Joseph," who played piano by ear and an aunt who sang light opera. We had a piano in the house. Both of my grandmothers had pianos, but there weren't any real musicians in the family.

What influenced you to become a drummer?
Well, I've heard this story but I don't know how true it is. My mother said that I was very slow in learning to walk. I was almost two years old and they were afraid that something was wrong with me. So my younger uncle, Lawrence Bagneris, his father got him a drum for his birthday and he started playing and I started walking.

And you know, New Orleans is full of music. Every Saturday or Sunday somebody would come down on a truck or a wagon and stop at a joint advertising a dance and you could hear the music. Music was all over.

When did you get your first drum?
I got my first drum when I was ten years old, in (Joseph A. Craig) grammar school.

A snare drum?
Yes. I was in the school band. We started out in grammar school and our music teacher used to come out once a week at night to instruct us. Can you believe that?

Every drummer that I have interviewed from New Orleans has cited their school music teachers as being their first influence.
We used to play at somebody's parents' house and she would come whenever one of them had a piano.

What school did you go to next?
High school, Xavier Prep. Benny Powell (trombonist with Thad Jones, Mel Lewis, Count Basie, etc.) and I went to school together.

Did you take lessons in school?
I took lessons two ways: in school with Miss Duvignea, and my professional teacher was Sydney Montegue who was the best technician in New Orleans. They used to call him "Beffy."

What did he show you?
Rudiments, marches, and regular reading. He used to play for the WPA (Works Projects Administration) band in the parks during the summer months. And they would play "Post and Pheasant" and Sousa marches and those kind of things. But he was also a jazz drummer. He was called whenever they needed a technician to play a show or something. He was my first professional teacher. But my first teacher was Miss Duvignea in grammar school.

She taught you how to read music, note values, etc.
Well, the main thing at that time was the rudiments. The first thing a guy would ask you

if you said you were a drummer was to play your rudiments, all of them. If you played them all, then you were a drummer. The first thing I learned was a press roll because that is the basis of New Orleans drumming.

Who did you learn that from?

Sydney. I used to go to his house on Saturday morning and I would wake him up around eleven o'clock, because he was a working musician, and we'd go in the kitchen, make coffee, he'd sit me down and make me press roll for about a half hour. Then he would say "O.K., go home." He did that for three or four Saturdays. He had a great press roll.

What's the key to a good press roll?

The key to a good press roll is the press. How to press on the head so you have just enough beats. You can get anywhere from five to eleven to thirteen beats according to how hard you press. The amount of pressure is very important. Most people don't know how to press roll. The real dixie was the press roll.

Was Paul Barbarin one of your main influences?

Yeah, one of the first ones. He wasn't my teacher but he was my first main influence. He was with the Sidney Desvigne band, one of the best bands in the country. (Alumni for this band included trumpeter Red Allen, singer/clarinetist Walter Pichon, and Johnny St. Cyr. banjo.)

In the 1930s?

I remember it from the early '40s, but they were around way before that. They were a dance band. We used to have bands come in here every Sunday, big bands like Count Basie and Duke Ellington, and there was a union rule that a local band had to play before them. Desvigne was the band that did that until the band that I was in, The Young Swingsters, got better and then we started doing it. We were teenagers, like fifteen, sixteen years old. Dooky Chase's Young Swingsters.

When did you first see Paul Barbarin play?

Maybe on a truck or a wagon the first time I went to a dance. Dances started early, around eight or nine o'clock, and you could stand outside. I first saw Paul Barbarin with Sidney Desvigne—that was his gig. He might go out of town with Louie (Armstrong), he was very in demand. He had so much work in New Orleans that he would never leave. He might go out of town for two or three months and then he would come back. He was the man.

How much older was he than you?

I was a teenager, so Paul must have been forty-something. He must have been around thirty years older than me.

What was your first professional gig?

My first professional gig was with Dooky Chase and the Young Swingsters. Our mothers and fathers were in the clubs and they would get us to play. We got so good that people started hiring us.

Outside of that, my first professional gig was with Adam Cato at the Old Absinthe

Vernel Fournier

House. I was about fifteen, I was in high school. I had to have a union card. When bebop came in, we had a little group and we used to play at Valenti's, Tony Valenti's on Bourbon street. We worked on Saturday and Sunday.

What kind of tunes were you playing?

Bebop. My first bebop influence was Art Blakey with the Billy Eckstine band.

Did he come through New Orleans?

Sure, Billy Eckstine used to come through New Orleans every two or three months. He had a very popular band.

How old were you the first time you saw Art?

Fourteen or fifteen.

Was his style radically different from what you were hearing around town?

Art and Paul [Barbarin] were similar except that Art was a little more modern. Art gave us what I call a lot of standard beats that a drummer has to play whether he knows it or not. If you listen to the old records like *Second Balcony Jump,* you hear things that he played on those records that guys still play. He had about fifteen or twenty things that he did that everybody had to play.

At the time we had the Young Swingsters, guys used to help us out like John "Picket" Brunious (trumpet player and nephew of Paul Barbarin), who took such an interest in us that he started writing arrangements for us.

He was much older than all of us. At that time you could also buy "stocks" (stock arrangements). For seventy-five cents you could buy Glenn Miller stocks, or Lionel Hampton, Duke Ellington, tunes like "One O'clock Jump."

In New Orleans, if people found out you wanted to be a musician they all would help. Guys would give you a lesson for twenty-five cents or fifteen cents. You had to pay a little something just so they were sure you were serious. Everybody helped.

How big were the groups that you were playing in?

At the beginning, we had no bass or piano, so there were seven or eight pieces in the Young Swingsters and it grew to seventeen, eighteen pieces. So I played with big bands all my life except when I played with Adam Cato on Bourbon Street and with Harold Dejan.

Where did you get your brush technique?

I got my brush styles from playing with Ahmad (Jamal). I never played brushes before working with him.

When did you leave New Orleans?

I left New Orleans in 1946. I went to Alabama State Teachers College. That was the first major musical college. The Erskine Hawkins band came out of there, they left before they even graduated because they were so good. They became the number one band in the country. I went there for a year and played

Ed Blackwell, Vernel Fournier, Earl Palmer

with their big band. I left school the second semester of my second year and went with King Kolax, which was another big band. So I played with big bands basically until I was twenty years old.

How did you get the gig with King Kolax?

Well, Benny Powell was with the band and they needed a drummer so they called me at school.

And then you went to Chicago with him?

No we got stranded in Oklahoma City. We were stranded there for almost a year, then I went home. Then King Kolax called me to come up to Chicago where he lived and to play with his quintet in 1948.

Did he have a house gig there?

Well, you know how it goes, two weeks and two weeks notice. You might end up staying there a year. If they didn't fire you at the beginning of the week that meant that you had at least two more weeks.

How long did you stay with him?

On and off for a year.

When you got to Chicago, did things go well for you? Did other drummers start to take notice of you?

Man, there were so many great drummers in Chicago that I wanted to go home the second day I was there!

One time I had a dance gig with Kolax and this guy comes up and says, "Hey man, I want to play something." So, I looked at the band and they said "Yeah, let him play." So, we had a way to switch, which guys don't do anymore—

While you were playing?

Yeah. I get up and I'm still playing the cymbal and the guy sits down and takes his left hand and starts playing. This guy plays his butt off and I hadn't heard him, I had heard all the other drummers, like Ike Day and all those other cats who scared the hell out of me. So when it was over the guy went around and got a half dollar from some of the guys and a quarter from me, and I asked the guys who was that, and they said, "Wilbur Ware, the bass player!"

Chicago had Ike Day, Dorell Anderson, Wesley Landers . . . countless other great drummers.

Tell me about Ike Day.

Ike Day was one of the baddest drummers I ever heard.

Who did he sound like?

Who did he sound like? Like nobody, like himself. He had his own thing going, he was a swinger. He wasn't about a lot of coordination; he could do it, but he was a swinger. He's the cat that inspired me to play music. He had his problems and I was always working so he used to stop by the crib and if he was tired or hungry I would fix him supper.

Was he older than you?

Not too much, a couple of years.

He was from Chicago?

Maywood, Illinois.

Is he still living?

He died when he was in his early thirties. There is a story from Africa that if you were the son of the king, you weren't automatically the king when the king died, it's whoever got the three-legged stool. And I had his stool when he died. He had pawned it to me. Somebody stole it and it hurt me in my heart. Ike Day was a master.

Who did he play with?

Well, there is only one thing out, if you can find it, with Gene Ammons. He was on a couple of sides with him but he played with everybody. Everybody was glad to see Ike, he was one of those kind of cats.

Do you think that there was a real Chicago sound in the drummers who played there?

Yeah, yeah.

What made that sound?

Swing.

Do you think that the Chicago sound was based on the New Orleans drummers who had moved there, including Baby Dodds, Zutty Singleton, Tubby Hall . . .

Could be, I don't know. I'm not too hip to Baby Dodds, because once I heard bebop I left dixie alone. I was busy trying to get into the scene. You had to play Max [Roach's] things because if you were rehearsing a group the alto player played like Bird [Charlie Parker], the piano player played like Bud [Powell], so the drummer had to play like Max. At least for the first two choruses. If the piano player played Bud's solo you had to play what Max played with Bud's solo. After that you could do something else, that was different.

Once I heard Art Blakey it cancelled out everything, but it was easy to make the transfer because Art Blakey was just a modern Paul Barbarin.

A big wide beat.

A big wide beat and an aggressive sound. You never heard the Billy Eckstine band?

No, but I know that it was very important to Art's development.

That was the *only* band. When Billy Eckstine came on the scene he wiped out everybody. He used to pack 'em in.

Did you listen to a lot of records at this time?

I didn't listen to a lot of records in Chicago because it was all there. See, Chicago was the kind of city where if John Coltrane, for instance, left New York and somebody cancelled out on him, the drummer or whomever, and he was going to Chicago, he didn't worry about nothing: in Chicago he knew he could pick up somebody to replace the drummer who was just as good or better.

Chicago was the kind of city, that years ago, they used to say, "You learn your craft in whatever city you're born in and you sharpen your craft in Chicago." Everybody used to come to Chicago from Alabama, Mississippi, and so on. Only the cats on the East coast went to New York. Everybody that left Chicago to go to New York had no problems that I know of. Not in the '40s, anyway.

You were well prepared.

Well prepared. The music was written in Chicago, really.

Were there any sides you recorded before Ahmad Jamal?

Most of my things before Ahmad were rock-and-roll things. I was a rock and roll studio drummer. The Dells, the Spaniards, the Oreos. When I got with Ahmad I had to put it down, 'cause Ahmad's thing was too demanding. When I got with Ahmad, he must have had 50 or 60 different arrangements of different tunes. So I couldn't fool with the rock thing, because with rock and roll you had to rehearse all day and record the following day and it took up too much time.

Were you playing beats from New Orleans on the rock dates?

Well, I guess so, the bass drum thing. That's the difference between New Orleans drummers and most other drummers—the use of the bass drum.

What does that mean specifically, where you play the bass drum or using dynamics?

Using dynamics, using syncopation. You said

you've been to New Orleans? Well, it comes from the street bands, the bass drum. That's where it comes from.

Where did Ahmad hear you?

I really don't know. The first time he called me I was working at the Beehive in Chicago.

You played in the house band at the Beehive?

Yeah, for over a year with Norman Simmons and Victor Sproles. That was my greatest time. I worked with Lester Young, Ben Webster, Sonny Stitt, J.J. Johnson, Kai Winding, Red Rodney and many others.

So you joined Ahmad in 1956?

'56 or '57. The first time he asked me I was busy at the Beehive, so Walter Perkins was his first drummer. And when Walter left he asked me again and then I joined. I had done trio work with Norman and I had a couple of things out with him, and I did a couple of things with Lorez Alexander, big hits. *Lorez Sings Prez.* In fact, she mentions my name on there, she says, "Vernel Fournier has something to say."

Where was Ahmad working?

All around town. First he came in with four strings, violin, guitar, bass and piano. Then he started using a drummer, which was Walter Perkins.

When you started playing in the trio after Walter, did you have to play the style that he had established—did you adapt your style?

Did I have to play like Walter? Naw. It was never like that when I was coming up. A guy hired you because he liked what you were playing.

I want to read you a quote from Modern Drummer *Magazine (June, 1995) with Jack DeJohnette on the cover. This is Jack talking about his work in the Keith Jarrett trio with bassist Gary Peacock: "We had all been influenced by the Ahmad Jamal Trio with Vernel Fournier on drums. In fact, that's what got me into drumming."*

Well, you know, Jack DeJohnette is a piano player. He played with Eddie Harris, that's when I first met him. I used to see him when I was in Chicago with Ahmad. When he started playing drums I used to kid him and say, "Man, you're making it hard for drummers." A guy needed a piano player, he would hire Jack DeJohnette, and when he needed a drummer he would hire Jack DeJohnette. Or if he had a sad piano player he might hire DeJohnette on drums, figuring he might need him on piano. He is one of the few cats that ever mentions me as an influence.

You know, if Jack DeJohnette is saying that the reason he played drums is because of you, think of all the people he has gone on to influence . . .

Well, a lot of cats tell me that personally, but they never say it in print. Like that magazine, they've never asked me to do anything with them. See, I stopped reading these magazines 25, 30 years ago when *Down Beat* magazine came out with a statement that it was best for musicians not to read music, but to play by ear. Who started that shit? I put it down. The only way I got in *Metronome* was because Shelly Manne—God bless his soul—recommended me and I got about five votes, and I was with the top trio in the country! "Poinciana" was the biggest thing out there. Not a drummer in the world that doesn't know anything about "Poinciana."

It seems impossible . . .

Well, I know the reason, and I hope that you are broad enough in your mind to understand what I'm trying to tell you. When I was with Ahmad, we were at the top of the ladder. There was prejudice and racism, there still is, but not like it was, and how did it look for a guy who *could* pass for white but who was black. [Vernel's grandmother was French, his grandfather, Haitian] It's just the opposite of the American situation. You never saw any pictures of me, did you? I tell you, no one in New York knew me. Except for a few old timers.

And then when I started playing sticks, they never gave me any recognition for playing sticks.

I always thought that on "Poinciana," you played the off-beats with the back end of your wire brush.

No, that was a stick. The back end of a stick.

On the bell?

On the bell.

And a mallet in your right hand going from the snare to the floor tom with your snares off.

Right. Just like [a bass drummer] in New Orleans. The only thing different was that the bass drummer couldn't make the rim shots.

So how did the beat come about?

I had just joined the band and we were playing the London House in Chicago. We were the house band, so I was playing intermission and I was re-adjusting the drums. And Ahmad started playing "Poinciana," so I just sat down and figured something out, you know, and it evolved. All it is, is New Orleans beats. You've seen the drummers in New Orleans with the bass drum and the cymbal on top, that's all it is. I found that out twenty years later. That's where it came from. The rest of it is another story, because you don't want to be doing the same damn thing over and over again. I never did believe in that, I always try to improve. Ahmad had one chorus, then another, and another and before you knew it we had six or seven choruses we could play that were all different. We could play that tune for ten, fifteen, twenty minutes.

Arranged choruses.

Well, most of his stuff was arranged.

How did you approach arranging the tunes as a trio?

Most of the things he had done before, he had a book when I got there. All I had to was find out what to play. The rest of it was like, say I'm playing with [pianist] Pete [Malinverni] tonight, and he plays something and he plays it again and I hear it and I add something to it, then we got a little thing going that we can use. Just rapport, listening to one another. Appreciating one another. If he plays something, I try to play something with him. I'm not trying to be me all the way. I'm Pete when he's playing, then the next guy that plays, I'm him. The bass player plays, I'm the bass player. And then when I play, I'm me. You understand what I'm saying? You enhance one another. You don't try to out-play one another, that doesn't make sense.

Vernel teaching in Chicago

It's a conversation.

Somewhat. I always said that a drummer is like the editor, putting the exclamation point, question mark, the colons, commas, underline, that's a drummer's job. Stay out of the way. Somewhere along the way he [the soloist] is going to run out of conversation and you fill it in until he gets himself together again. Sometimes when I was with Ahmad we'd be playing and he would rest awhile. We'd vamp until he got his second wind. And then we'd try it again, then if he didn't make it in one chorus we'd go somewhere else. And if he makes it, we might be able to play five or six more choruses besides the ten he played before. But they are all interesting. It is not just a horse race all the way. That's what I learned from Ahmad.

You said before that you developed your brush technique with Ahmad.

Well, like I said before, you don't settle for anything because you are playing brushes, you keep trying to improve, you learn this,

you learn that, next thing you know . . . See, I was with Ahmad from 1957 to 1960 and all I did was play brushes. The only time I touched a stick was for "Poinciana." So I had to learn how to do things to keep myself interested in what was going on. I learned different grooves, different ways to do the brushes, different sounds, and improved on them. If you had to play brushes for three years and you are really interested in playing, you'll come up with a lot of things.

We were playing on the same bill with Dave Brubeck in Cleveland and Dave was hot at the time, but Ahmad was hotter. Dave had Paul Desmond, Joe Morello and a bass player from Chicago. Anyway, they were bearing down! So we get up there and we got into another chorus, or the bridge, and Ahmad looks over at me and yells, "Sticks," and luckily I kept sticks on the drum because of "Poinciana." So that was the first time I played sticks with Ahmad. Dave Brubeck was the cause of me playing sticks. Ain't that something! Then it got to the point where I was playing sticks 70% of the time.

Vernel Fournier

What kind of drums were you playing with Ahmad?

Ludwig, always Ludwig.

With calf heads?

Always calf heads.

What size was your bass drum?

In the early days I had a 22" or 24", then I went down to twenty, that's the lowest I ever got. If the drum is smaller than a twenty the pedal hits too high up on the head and you can't get any tone. With a 20" you hit just above the center. With a 22" or 24", you hit right in the center.

With Ahmad you used a 22" or 24"?

I believe so. Ludwig gave me some drums. I've always been commercial, so every year they wanted to give me a set of drums. So I told them, instead of giving me these drums every year why don't you give me some money, because it takes a long time to break in drums. They don't realize that. So the guy says, "The only people we give money to are Buddy Rich and Joe Morello."

In the video [Jazz Masters Vintage Collection Vol. 2: 1960–61], you play with a floor tom but no mounted tom.

If I didn't have it with me I didn't use it. Guys didn't use a lot of drums in those days. Now guys have four toms up there and twenty cymbals. I had two cymbals.

Tell us about those cymbals. Did you like them dry?

Heavy, heavy 20". They used to call it "band" weight. I found one used in Chicago and Lester Young fell in love with it, so I kept it.

Did you ever use a china-type cymbal?

At one time, because of Art Blakey. He had one with the Billy Eckstine band.

How big were the hi-hat cymbals you were using?

15" hi-hats. A 16" or 18" on the left side and a 20" on the right.

Who did you work with after Ahmad?

George Shearing for two years. I learned a lot from George. I made the statement once that I learned a lot of control and finesse from George. His stuff was all set, he wasn't as free as Ahmad.

That was a big deal when he put out a record and across the cover was The George Shearing Trio featuring Vernel Fournier on drums and the late great bassist, Israel Crosby (Capitol).

He played some hard things on that record, things in 9/4, 5/4, 7/4. I love George, I bought my first home when I was working with him. He gave me half-salary when I was off.

When Ahmad's band broke up the first time, he hired Israel and I together as a team. I stayed with him two years. Then I worked at Mr. Kellys in Chicago. I worked with Bill Cosby, Totie Fields, with Ernie Knovac, a Polish piano player. He could play his ass off. I have a CD around here somewhere that we did. I did that for a year, then I went back with Ahmad and I was with him for about six or seven months and I got a call from Nancy Wilson—one of those offers I couldn't refuse.

Another great aspect of your playing is where you place your bass drum accents.

Well, you just wait for the opportunity. I listen to the tunes and I find the best spots to accent the tune, not to enhance me. If I please Pete, I work. If I please [another drummer], it doesn't do me any good. If I please Pete it helps him, and that helps him with the people.

You have to make the people you work with sound good.

As best I can.

*From 1967 to 1979, Vernel led a trio with Willie Pickins, and later John Young, on piano and Eddie Calhoun on bass, at the Shalom restaurant (owned by Elijah Muhammad) in Chicago. In 1979, Vernel moved to New York. In addition to recording three albums with Clifford Jordan (*Repetition, Royal Ballads, *and* Clifford Jordan Big Band Live at Condon's*), Vernel has also performed with Joe Williams, Harry Edison, Barry Harris, John Lewis, Dick Katz, Pepper Adams and Billy Eckstine. In 1987 he reunited with Ahmad Jamal at Umbria Jazz in Perugia, Italy, for a ten-day engagement. In 1991 he appeared in concert at New York's City College along with Earl Palmer and the late Ed Blackwell, demonstrating New Orleans drum technique.*

His CD, entitled The Vernel Fournier Trio *(TCB Records), was released in 1991 and features a number of Vernel's own compositions. Before suffering a stroke in 1993, Vernel was also an active educator and taught at the Barry Harris Cultural Theatre, the New School, and Mannes College of Music in New York. Extensive rehabilitative therapy has helped Vernel greatly, and he expects to resume teaching and playing in the near future.*

VERNEL FOURNIER SELECTED DISCOGRAPHY

Lorez Alexander *Lorez Sings Perez, This is Lorez;* **Billy Eckstine** (Japanese release); **Vernel Fournier Trio** (TCB Records); **Wardell Gray** *Easy Swing* (Swingtime); **Ahmad Jamal** *Blackhawk, The Spotlight, Poinciana* (Chess), *Jamal At The Pershing, Vol. 2* (Cadet), *Ahmad's Blues* (Jazz Society), *Live at the Alhambra* (Vogue); **Etta Jones** *I'll Be Seeing You* (Muse); **Sam Jones** *The Riverside Collection: Sam Jones—Right Down Front* (Original Jazz Classics); **Clifford Jordan** *Repetition* (Soul Note), *Royal Ballads* (Criss Cross); **George Shearing** *Jazz Moments* (Capitol), *Live in Santa Monica*; **Red Hot Peppers** *New Orleans* (Horn Records, Switzerland)

This video, Jazzmasters, Vintage Collection Vol. 2: 1960–61, contains two songs with the classic Ahmad Jamal Trio. Highly Recommended. Available from Warner Bros. Publications, Inc., 1-800-628-1528 ext. 215/214.

The Drum and Dance are One

"He listens so intensely to everybody that he plays with. He makes what they play sound better. People come up to me after we play and tell me how great I sound and I say, 'Well, it's Blackwell.' As long as Blackwell is playing, I just have to hold the bass—and he plays it for me."

*—Charlie Haden
Interview with Kalamu ya Salaam, Coda Magazine*

"I was from a section called the Garden District. New Orleans was separated into different sections, like front-of-town, back-of-town, downtown, uptown, instead of north, south, east and west. And my section was called the Garden District. The most popular nightclub at that time was called the Dew Drop Inn and we used to play there quite a bit, but we also played for vaudeville acts—tap dancers, belly dancers, fire dancers, vocalists, shake dancers—and that was my schooling of experience."

—Blackwell

In New Orleans, music is an integral part of everyday life. Drumming in particular is commonly heard in the wards, or neighborhoods, of the city and serves the same purpose as in the African tradition: to call attention to a special event and to bring people together. Ed Blackwell absorbed the feeling and energy of New Orleans parade music at an early age:

> *When I was a kid, every Sunday there was a parade. There was a parade for funerals, births, deaths. Everything called for a parade. In a minute, people would get out and start playing a parade. Naturally, when you heard the music, people would gather and a big crowd would just follow behind . . .You could hear the bass drum coming and you knew it was a parade. All the kids would have the "second line." The kids would follow behind the parade, dancing. Most of the drummers would come up with that heritage, and you can hear it in their playing.*[1]

Blackwell was influenced by many New Orleans drummers, but of particular note was Wilber Hogan, who went on to play with Ray Charles.

> *Wilber was about three grades ahead of me in school, and when I went to high school I wanted to play in the band but I couldn't read. So he volunteered to teach me to read the music, so the teacher accepted me as a drummer in the high school band . . . . Wilber was the one that first taught me about the rudiments, and the paradiddles, and all the basics of the drums.*[2]

Another New Orleans drummer who influenced Blackwell's sound was Paul Barbarin. Barbarin had played with King Oliver and Louis Armstrong and was of the generation of drummers whose careers coincided with the development of the modern drumset. The two met at a club where Barbarin played in a Dixieland band and Blackwell had an after-hours gig. Blackwell recalled, "I used to go down [to the club] early and I'd sit down and [he would] talk to me a lot about the drums and drum rolls, how he played and how he learned to play."[3]

A neighbor who had heard him practicing recommended Ed Blackwell for his first professional gig, with the Johnson Brothers in 1949, a group that played popular R&B tunes and shuffles. Blackwell, who neither owned nor had played a full drumset before, improvised a set that included a 16" military snare which he converted to a bass drum, and a tenor drum with legs added to make a floor tom. These drums, close in pitch, may have been the genesis of the classic Blackwell sound: relatively high tunings with open, but clear and controlled, tones from all the drums. Later in life Blackwell would relate his drumset to the African concept of a drum "family," with the bass drum as the "papa," the floor tom as the mother, and the mounted tom and snare as the "kids." He also made his own stick mallets in order to enhance his melodic style.

In 1951 Blackwell decided to move to California. His travelling companion was another well-known New Orleans musician, pianist Ellis Marsalis. Marsalis remembers the trip:

> *It was a long ride. Very long. And we didn't have much money, in fact, I don't know if we had any. What Blackwell would do, he would play the snare drum. He had a snare drum on his lap. And he knew all these Charlie Parker songs and he would play them on the drums, sort of like "Name That Tune" as played by the drummer! Edward knew all the tunes so well and could articulate it on the drum so well that you'd have to be deaf not to hear it, I mean, he was just that precise in what he did.*[4]

Blackwell himself admitted, "That was my schooling, listening to Charlie Parker records—you know, "Dewey Square" and all his records on Dial . . . . [I knew the owner of a] drum shop, he used to order these records directly from New York for me . . . Even before they got to New Orleans on the radio, I would get them privately, you know."[5]

By 1953 Blackwell was sharing a room in Los Angeles with Ornette Coleman, whom he had met previously in New Orleans. Blackwell was one of the few players interested in Ornette's unorthodox approach to melody and form at the time. Both musicians worked day jobs at local department stores to pay the rent, ceaselessly conceptualizing and practicing during their off hours. The reaction to Ornette's music was disappointing, however, and in 1956, Blackwell returned to New Orleans.

For a year, Blackwell worked with R&B groups led by Roy Brown, Earl King and Huey "Piano" Smith, finally ending up touring with Ray Charles. 1958 found him back in New Orleans with the American Jazz Quintet, an ensemble led by clarinetist Alvin Batiste and Ellis Marsalis. An acknowledged master by this time, Blackwell's influence on the next generation of drummers was making itself felt. One of the most impressed was the young James Black:

> I used to go out to this place where Ed Blackwell, Ellis Marsalis, Chuck Badie and Nat Perrilliat used to play. I thought Blackwell was the greatest thing I'd ever heard. I said, "Wow! I never knew you could get all this out of the drums!" It made me go home and practice more![6]

Blackwell not only had a grooving swing feel rooted in R&B and refined in bebop, but was also a virtuoso soloist. Drummer and *Down Beat* correspondent Charles Suhor remembered hearing Blackwell at this time:

> Blackwell not only had prodigious technique and exceptional coordination, but he was the most inventive drummer I had ever heard. His solos, executed with what can only be described paradoxically as icy abandon, were gems of asymmetry. It was a challenging delight to follow Blackwell's lines down devious paths and then back again to home base. Even more refreshing was his instinct for deviating from standard practices at the right time to stimulate the soloist with ingenious devices that would be tasteless distractions or affectations in the hands of the less perceptive.[7]

Blackwell himself was always quick to credit Max Roach with influencing his melodic soloing style within the structure of a tune.

Meanwhile, Ornette Coleman was having much better luck in New York City than he had had in California, playing six nights a week to enthusiastic crowds at the Five Spot club. When legal troubles prevented his drummer from performing in cabarets, Ornette called Blackwell to step in. Blackwell had troubles of his own: he faced five years of hard labor in New Orleans for miscegenation (interracial marriage), but was permitted to leave town and went immediately to New York.

Blackwell attracted a lot of attention in New York not only because he could navigate the music of Ornette Coleman, but also because of his unique sound. Max Roach was one of many drummers who were awed by Blackwell's playing:

> I had first heard about Ed Blackwell from the musicians that were coming through New

Ed Blackwell

EDWARD BLACKWELL SELECTED DISCOGRAPHY

American Jazz Quintet *In The Beginning* (AFO Classic), *From Bad To Badder* (Black Saint); **Ray Anderson** *Every One Of Us* (Gramavision); **Bill Barron** *Jazz Caper* (Muse); **Jane Ira Bloom** *Mighty Lights* (Enja); **Karl Berger** *Transit* (Black Saint), *Crystal Fire* (Enja); **Anthony Braxton** *Six Compositions Quartet* (Antilles); **Don Cherry** *Mu (The Complete Session)* (Affinity), *El Corazón* (ECM), *Complete Communion* (Blue Note), *Symphony For Improvisers* (Blue Note), *Multi Kulti* (A&M); **Ornette Coleman** *Broken Shadows* (Columbia), *The Art Of The Improvisers, Ornette!, This Is Our Music, Free Jazz, Twins, Ornette On Tenor* (Atlantic), *Live In Milano, 1968* (Jazz Up), *Broken Shadows* (Moon), *The Unprecedented Music Of Ornette Coleman* (Lotus); **John Coltrane & Don Cherry** *The Avant-Garde* (Atlantic); **Eric Dolphy** *At The Five Spot Vol. 1, At The Five Spot Vol. 2, Memorial Album* (Original Jazz Classics); **Joe Lovano** *From The Soul* (Blue Note), *Sounds Of Joy* (Enja); **Donald Harrison** *Eric Dolphy & Booker Little Remembered* (Paddle Wheel); **David Murray Quartet** *Morning Song* (Black Saint); **Old And New Dreams** *Old And New Dreams, Playing* (ECM), *A Tribute To Blackwell* (Black Saint); **Dewey Redman** *Redman and Blackwell In Willisau* (Black Saint), *The Struggle Continues* (ECM); **Ed Blackwell Project** *What It Is?, What It Look Like?* (Enja); **Mal Waldron** *You And The Night And The Music* (Paddle Wheel), *The Seagulls Of Kristiansund* (Soul Note)

York City out of New Orleans. When I finally heard him, [he] was with Ornette, maybe even Don Cherry when they first came to New York. I had never heard a drummer who sounded like Ed. He had his own musical personality, and he had an approach to the instrument that was really captivating . . . He was an original, and when you're trying to make a name for yourself, being an original is a big boost for you because you can be identified immediately on records. Before I walked into a club, just by hearing him outside, I knew it was Ed. I think he made a great contribution to the instrument.[8]

Blackwell remained in New York until 1972 and appeared on a number of revolutionary recordings with Ornette Coleman, John Coltrane, Eric Dolphy, Booker Little and Don Cherry. His joyful, infectious second line feel set him apart from other drummers who were playing "modern" jazz in the '60s and '70s. As drumming styles became increasingly cerebral, Blackwell went the other way, into a soulful exploration of the African roots of his New Orleans heritage. His trips to Morocco and West Africa, the first of which was a State Department-sponsored tour with pianist Randy Weston in 1965, began an investigation into multiple rhythms and layers of time that continued until the end of his life.

Ed Blackwell publicity shot with The Ray Charles Band

In 1972, Blackwell became an Artist in Residence at Wesleyan University in Middletown, Connecticut, where he collaborated with Ghanaian master drummers Freeman Donkor, Abraham Adzenyah and others. Royal Hartigan, drummer, scholar and author of *West African Rhythms for Drumset* (1995: Manhattan Music Publications), studied under Blackwell during this period and was impressed by the spiritual quality of his playing. Hartigan recounts, "When I asked him how he did these great things on the drumset, Blackwell told me, 'I feel a Spirit dancing on the drums.'"

Although he continued to record through the '70s, '80s and '90s with artists such as Don Cherry, Charlie Haden, Old and New Dreams featuring Dewey Redman, and his own group, Ed Blackwell Project, with Graham Haynes, Carlos Ward, and bassist Mark Helias, Blackwell's health was deteriorating due to kidney disease and diabetes. He died October 7, 1992 at the age of 62, leaving a recorded legacy staggering in its originality and depth.

Royal Hartigan sums up Blackwell's compelling influence: "He didn't move around a lot as he played but if you close your eyes, you can hear his rhythms and tones as a dance on the drums and cymbals. West African music, New Orleans street bands and jazz all identify dance movements with drum rhythms, and Blackwell observed and participated in all three. Despite severe illness . . . he would get off his sick bed and go to a gig by sheer force of will. He willed himself above his own pain. He danced on the drumset in the same way he danced in life, overcoming both material need and physical infirmity to live the music that was the meaning of his life."[9]

SOURCES
1 *Ed Blackwell: Singin' On The Set,* by Scott Fish, *Modern Drummer,* November 1981.
2 Blackwell interview courtesy of Frances Blackwell.
3 *Ed Blackwell: Singin' On The Set,* by Scott Fish, *Modern Drummer,* November 1981.
4 *Blackwell,* Jazzset, National Public Radio, Sept. 9, 1993.
5 ibid.
6 *Back Home with James Black,* by Scott Fish, *Modern Drummer,* December 1982.
7 *New Jazz in the Cradle, Part II,* by Charles Suhor, *Down Beat* August 31, 1961.
8 *Blackwell,* Jazzset, National Public Radio, Sept. 9, 1993.
9 Royal Hartigan interview with Dan Thress, NYC, 1995.

JAMES BLACK

We've covered a lot of earlier jazz styles, but you're best known through the recordings of Wynton Marsalis, his father Ellis, the Lincoln Center Jazz Orchestra, and Ahmad Jamal. Where did your modern concepts come from? Were you influenced by drummers Ed Blackwell and James Black?

Those drummers played a lot in the '60s and '70s and as a child, I grew up hearing that style, mostly from my uncles, Melvin Lastie, David Lastie and Walter Lastie. They had a combo that they would rehearse at my grandmother's house where I was pretty much raised. I listened to them playing Fats Domino R&B stuff, and then they would play something like "Moanin'" by Art Blakey and the Jazz Messengers. So I heard those two styles and my grandfather was playing the earlier stuff. As I was growing up, all this music was around me all the time, so it was never a big deal going from one idiom to the other.

But as I grew older and I really started to investigate the music, I began to see where some of the more modern concepts were coming from, by hearing people like James Black, who was a big influence on my playing.

His name gets mentioned a lot down here in New Orleans.

Yeah, James was a phenomenal musician. He was a great drummer and also a great composer.

"MAGNOLIA TRIANGLE"

You're going to play one of his compositions in 5/4, right?

This is in 5/4, it's a composition he wrote called "Magnolia Triangle."

Originally, he played it with a swing feel. But I'm going to attempt to play it with a bit of a New Orleans kind of feeling on it with some press rolls inside the 5/4, to give you an idea of where the early parade bands have brought us thus far.

This tune has some really unique sections to it. Can you break those down for us?

OK, here's the intro:

CD TRACK 31

If you noticed, it still has the parade feel on the bass drum even though it's in 5/4.

Show us that move on the hi-hat.

OK.

CD TRACK 32

"Magnolia Triangle"

Main groove:

etc.

CD TRACK 33

DRUMS

Play 7

A

B

fine

Solos: Trumpet 2 choruses
    Piano 2 choruses
    Drum solo 1 chorus then open solo over vamp
    Out head 1x to fine

"Magnolia Triangle" Drum Solo

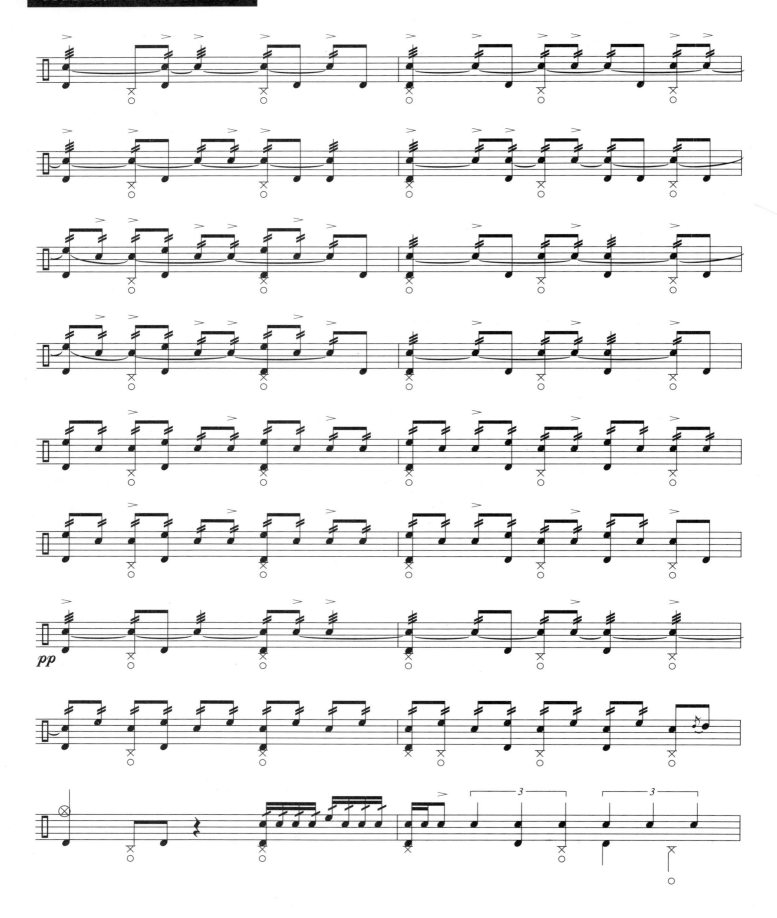

That's great. What did James Black's version sound like?

Well, James played all kinds of wild stuff inside of his version—his version was more swinging, like this:

CD TRACK 34

etc.

JAMES BLACK AND FREDDIE KOHLMAN
by Val Wilmer, August 1974

THIS ARTICLE ORIGINALLY APPEARED IN CODA MAGAZINE AUGUST 1975

New Orleans is one of the few remaining cities where it is still possible to take a kind of intensive course in listening by moving from one bar to another and checking out a wide variety of musical styles. In particular, the concentration of musical talent there and the frequent street parades provide a unique opportunity to study the drummers for which the city is famous. The Crescent City, after all, not only entered stalwart traditionalists like Baby Dodds and Paul Barbarin in the percussion stakes, it is also responsible for introducing the unique style of R&B drumming perpetuated by such players as Charles "Hungry" Williams and Cornelius "Tenoo" Coleman. And then there's Edward Blackwell, a complete original and innovator in his own right, who contributed enormously to the work of Ornette Coleman.

The two finest percussion artists playing today in New Orleans are—for my money—James Black and Freddie Kohlman. Black works weekends at Lu and Charlie's on Ursulines and Rampart with the ELM Music Quartet, a band led by pianist Ellis Marsalis. Kohlman leads his own group at Maison Bourbon in the heart of the French Quarter. Both men swing as though they invented the word and although separated by a quarter of a century in age, each personifies the virtually inimitable New Orleans beat.

James Black, born in 1940 in the Crescent City itself, came from a musical family. His first professional job came in 1958 with an R&B band, "somewhere out in the country. I remember as I was playing, I was slapping mosquitoes at the same time." He left school to work in the Playboy Club with Ellis Marsalis, and also worked for a while with tenor saxophonist Nat Perrilliat and guitarist Roy Montrell. He went to New York with the R&B pianist, Joe Jones, and from there, went on the road with Lionel Hampton. He played and recorded with Cannonball Adderley, Yusef Lateef and Horace Silver before

finally opting for the easy life provided by his home town. There he played with saxophonist James Rivers, and with Fats Domino and Professor Longhair for a while, although he never recorded with either performer. He did, however record with Lee Dorsey, Irma Thomas and the Meters, and for some time made all of Allen Toussaint's sessions. When he was studying music, Black played with Southern University's Marching Band, but has never, as yet, played a New Orleans parade. This is, however, one of the few omissions in his permanently hectic schedule.

Freddie Kohlman is equally busy when it comes to freelancing. Born in 1915 in Algiers, he studied with Louis Cottrell Sr., who was one of the acknowledged all-time greats among New Orleans drummers. His first job was with the Sam Morgan band and later he worked with Papa Celestin and Joe Robichaux. He spent 15 years in Chicago where he worked with Stuff Smith and Albert Ammons amongst others, and for three years, he was resident at Disneyland in Hollywood. Since returning home, he has played with just about everyone in the city, including the Dukes of Dixieland and several marching bands. He appeared on-stage with Punch Miller in the movie, "Till The Butcher Cut Him Down."

This is an edited transcript of a conversation with Black and Kohlman held at Lu and Charlie's one afternoon in August.

V.W.: New Orleans has always been a town for drummers, hasn't it?

F.K.: Well, drummers and clarinet players . . .

J.B.: Drummers!

F.K.: You get a lot of wonderful piano players, very few trombonists . . .

V.W.: Who did you listen to when you were coming up?

F.K.: Oh, like Baby Dodds, Big Sid Catlett. My teacher was old man Louis Cottrell. And I used to listen to Louis Barbarin when he was playing with Papa Celestin's big band.

J.B.: From the very beginning? Shelly Manne, Art Blakey, Philly Joe Jones, Max Roach. Of course, Elvin Jones. And what was that dude who played so nice on the cymbals all the time? He never did play too much but he played with Miles and them? You know the dude I'm talking about, man!

V.W.: Art Taylor?

J.B.: Art Taylor, yeah! He played the time and everything so beautifully. He never varied it too much. I used to like to hear him play the cymbals. He didn't, you know, go through all the Elvin Jones kind of thing with the excitement and polyrhythms and stuff, but he just kept the time going, kept a groove going, kept the whole thing swinging. I used to listen to that.

V.W.: What about the local drummers— did you listen to Freddie?

J.B.: Of course.

F.K.: Oh, we listened to each other!

J.B.: Ha, ha, listen at this!

F.K.: I used to hire him to work for me!

J.B.: Oh, I listened to Freddie, I listened to Louis, and there's some cats down there—I don't even know their names— but I used to listen to what they were doing. And of course, Ed Blackwell.

V.W.: You told me before—and I've heard it from other people too, how people like Berry Gordy used to come down to New Orleans looking for drummers because they couldn't get that beat anywhere else. Blackwell was talking about how it came from the parade bands. Although you're a little younger than him, James, did you follow the parades, too?

J.B.: Sure, everybody did, I guess—if they had any soul in them.

F.K.: Any youngster who was interested in music followed the parade. He picked the instrument that he wanted to play and he followed the guy that played that instrument. It's like I was crazy about drums; during my time as a kid, I used to follow Louis Cottrell's daddy. He used to play the snare drum in the parade and I always wanted to be the snare drum player in the parade band because the way he played was so beautiful. I got the opportunity to play in a parade when Red Allen's daddy had a brass band, old man Henry Allen. He hired me one day to play a parade and that was the greatest thing in my life. I was about 13, 14 years old.

V.W.: But you've never played any parade, James?

J.B.: Never have. I doubt that I will, but who knows . . .

F.K.: You never can tell what you're going to do in this kind of music in New Orleans. You might say "I'm never going to play a parade," then all of a sudden the urge will hit you and you'll say "Oh, I think I'll try."

J.B.: It's not the urge—I've never been hired!

F.K.: Well, if a guy would hire you, you might get the urge just like I did. Now, they've switched me to bass drum in the Onward Brass Band. I don't prefer to play bass drum, but I said I'll try it. Now I play it all the time.

J.B.: Well, if they need a snare drummer, call me.

F.K.: All right!

V.W.: Do the kids still follow the one musician they like, Freddie?

F.K.: Oh yes, you have kids come up and ask you questions. A lot of kids play in the school bands, too, and they want to get the idea of playing in a regular street band. The way they're playing, the things they're playing in that school band, is much different from what we're doing in the street.

J.B.: It ain't that much different.

F.K.: It's a whole lot different, James— really. The teacher's writing everything for them and they're playing it right there. But (to get that) beat, you've got to get it out in the street with one of them brass bands (and listen to) especially the bass drum. That's where all that footwork comes from—the New Orleans style of playing it with their hands. That's why New Orleans drummers got it over all the different cats that are away from here because of their foot and the way they play that parade beat on a lot of them rock tunes.

J.B.: That's it, now I know why. I agree with that one hundred percent.

V.W.: Do you think it has also something to do with the fact that while the traditional jazz—I don't want to use the 'Dixieland'—

J.B.: Traditional Black Music . . .

V.W.: . . . continued, there was also a lot of blues here, wasn't there?

F.K.: Yes, that had a whole lot to do with it. You had guys that would play around here in the olden days at what you'd call 'fish-frys'. They would walk in where there was a piano in the house and start playing the blues, and you'd see everybody walking in just to watch this piano player. They used to call them 'Saturday night fish-frys' then, but it's 'Suppers' today. Every time you'd see a little red lantern out in front of a house, you'd say "Oh, somebody got a fish-fry tonight."

V.W.: And anybody could go?

F.K.: Anybody could go in there and they would sell them homebrew or homemade beer—that's alcohol and water mixed up—and you could get a fish sandwich or a chicken supper or whatever you want.

V.W.: You mentioned the connection between the parades and tough footwork, but James, you said you hadn't thought of that before . . .

J.B.: Yeah, I'd thought about that. I said "now where is all this coming from?" I set out there doing my historical research and I said "well, yeah, this is the parade town." There's no other city in the United States that has Second Lines and jazz funerals and just partying Second Lines where they say like "we're going to give a parade," and they get together with their umbrellas and stuff and boom—there it is! No funeral, nothing—just a whole bunch of fun. I guess it's just like a thing you grow up with naturally. Like Freddie was saying— well, he brought it from the origins, whereas I can only dig it from where it is now. But when you go to any dance like I played for when I was a kid coming up, you had to play the Second Line in

Freddie Kohlman playing with the Onward Brass Band in 1972.

the dance. If you didn't play the Second Line, you didn't have no kind of band.

V.W.: I was talking to Justin Adams, the guitarist, and he said that in Los Angeles they would have like three drummers to do the thing that one person could do down here.

J.B.: I don't know what to say about that, but I guess it's just a natural outgrowth of the Second Line. It's sort of our foundation. With the infectious dance beat that the Second Line evokes, quite naturally it has evolved into a different sort of rhythm which would be the rhythm of today, the rhythm of this generation. I think the drummer tried to encompass or draw from and play everything that the whole percussion section played in the parade, and he just did it quite naturally because of the 'natural rhythm', I guess you'd call it.

I came up like that, but the rest of the country doesn't have this sort of parade background and so they didn't have this to draw from. This experience, this knowledge, was all around you just to draw from—sort of like fertile ground. It was just rich, Black ground. We just evolved our own particular beat which contained the Second Line—a dancing, marching, strutting sort of step or beat.

F.K.: I'll tell you an incident that happened in Chicago when I was there. The Impressions and Barbara Lewis were making a record together and they couldn't get his drummer to play exactly what they wanted. Some guy told the guy who was making the record: "I know a drummer from New Orleans, he could tell this drummer exactly where the beat goes that we want to hear." So they called me up and I went down to the studio and he said, "Freddie, look—you come from New Orleans. You tell the drummer the New Orleans beat." So I sat down and I said, "Well, look, man— all I'm playing now is Dixieland. I know what you want and I can show him." I sat down there and I played a parade beat and the man jumped up and he said, "That's it! That's what I want— exactly!" And he gave me 150 dollars just for showing the other drummer the beat.

J.B.: It amazes me to leave away from here and for somebody to say, "Yeah, I want you to play that New Orleans beat." It's like a thing that we just take for granted, for natural, and if you stop to think "Now, what would he really want?"

you get carried away into something else. But if you just sit down and let go and just play from where you're coming from, you can't go no further.

F.K.: It's a thing that the New Orleans drummers have got. It's a thing that James got, that I've got, it's a thing that all the rest of the drummers got—that the Northern drummers don't have and they wish they had it.

J.B.: I notice that. More and more I'm beginning to realize that.

F.K.: Whenever you go anywhere and say you're from New Orleans, the first thing they say is "You got that New Orleans beat, huh?" I'll tell you who started all that mess, man, it was Fats Domino when he brought "Tenoo" out there with him. That was Cornelius Coleman—he died but when Fats went away from here, everybody wanted that beat. And when I was in Chicago, even the guys there would say, "Man, I want that Fats Domino beat"—even on the recordings. But what they were talking about was "Tenoo" with that drum.

J.B.: Yes, I forgot to mention him, too.

F.K.: Fats was hot at the time and 'Tenoo' was wailin' on him and putting that foot down on that bass drum, and that's all they wanted. They didn't care what he was doing with the hands as long as they could hear that bass drum. And the only thing he was doing was what he saw those guys out in the street doing. He was doing it with his foot— just like James doing that thing with his foot. I play with a Dixieland band, but I sneak in something now and then— which they like!

V.W.: Somebody suggested that it was in New Orleans that the trap drums were first fitted together, that when they played in the pit bands in the theatres, there wasn't much space and so the small tom-tom was fixed on to the bass drum.

F.K.: Well, my teacher, Louis Cottrell Senior, played in a pit band and he was a helluva drummer. Man, he could make a roll sound like a window-shade— sh-sh-sh-sh-sh-sh-sh-p! That was the first drummer I saw in my life sitting up there with everything around him—chimes, vibraphone, xylophone, marimbas and everything. Back in those days, if drummers had to play a show, they had to have the different effects— boat whistles and everything. They were real percussionists!

They used to have a theater called the Lyric Theatre on the corner of Iberville and Burgundy and all the big Black acts used to come there, Butterbeans and Susie, Bessie Smith—all the black vaudeville acts. The Palace was on another corner with all white acts and an all-white band and they had shows at the Lyric as big as they had at the Palace Theatre. Old man Cottrell was the drummer at the Lyric and on a Sunday afternoon, my mother would give me money to go see the show. I'd sit right in front of the drummer, I wanted to see him use all that stuff. He used to tell my mother, "Let him come to the theatre and see me playing these things, and he can learn what's going on."

Old man Robichaux was the band leader there. He had about twenty pieces down there, violins and cats playing the whole works. And people would come down there and bring charts from here to way across the street! Some of the acts would bring their own drummer with them. There used to be two comedians that were out of sight, they used to call 'em "Hot Tamale" and "Chili Con Carne." The drummer used to have a bucket hanging behind him with a piece of rope full of rosin attached to a piece of leather. He'd pull that leather on that rope, and it'd sound like a lion's roar—"grrr! grrr!'" That would knock you out. Roy Evans was the name of the drummer who did that. And in those days, too, some of the drummers would carry their own valet to set up their traps.

J.B.: Why'd they call 'em traps?

F.K.: It came from the bass drum pedal. The oldtime bass drum pedal used to hook on the rim of the drum and it had like a slat come down and that had a hinge on it. In the middle was a ball, and then where you put your foot they had another slat with a hinge where the piece came up and they used to call it a "trap." It was (fixed with) two pieces of leather and you put your foot in the "trap."

J.B.: Do you remember those—now, I've seen pictures of them—the backwards beater that you play with your heel instead of your toe?

F.K.: Yeah, that was a "trap."

J.B.: But who was the first person to fit together the snare and the bass drum?

F.K.: The first person that I ever saw do that was old man Cottrell. And I'll tell you, he had a set of folding drums, too. Did you ever see that?

J.B.: Explain that to me!

F.K.: The bass drum was made with legs and everything, but when you got ready to break it down, you could fold it up because it had hinges. You'd take the head off. The shell was round, with two hinges and on the other side was a piece of wood. My mother tried to buy the set when he died. The snare drum was the same thing. It was a wooden shell—they wasn't making metal shells in those days.

J.B.: But what about before that, when did cats start playing bass drum with a pedal instead of with their hands?

F.K.: Oh, I've heard of guys talking about where they had two drummers in the band—one played snare drum and the other played bass drum—and that was back in the "twenties." A guy like Chris Kelly—he was a helluva trumpet player—he would have two guys like that.

Before tom-toms came out, I used to have a set of drums that had a little Chinese tom-tom that used to hook on to the side of the bass drum. There used to be a ring hook on it and there was a little piece that curved around like the tom-tom, and you could set it right in there and it'd hold up so you could set it at any angle you wanted. Then they started making the floor tom-tom that was round with pigskin on it and little tacks all around the side. You couldn't tune it up and when the weather got bad, it went flat.

I started out playing the snare drum and when I wanted to play the whole set I used to go up on the roof-garden where old man Cottrell had his drums. He started me into playing the two drums then—the bass drum and the snare drum. I didn't even know how to work the hi-hat because in those days they were making hi-hats just a little off the floor. It was on a metal stand but it was short. I didn't know nothing about beating on no hi-hat—All I knew was it just kept for the after-beat on time. In later years, they came up high, but they didn't call them hi-hats then, they called 'em floor cymbals.

When I started—this might sound funny to you—right on my beater there was a little thing that looked like a ball but was a solid piece of metal. On the right-hand side of the bass drum there was a cymbal, and when you hit the bass drum, you'd hit that cymbal on the side, too, and you'd hear "boom-ching,"

"boom-ching," "boom-ching." That was what the drummers used when I started—that little Chinese tom-tom, one cymbal, one snare drum, one bass drum, one foot-pedal—didn't even have the floor cymbal then. I got all confused when I started with that, trying to make that after-beat. When hi-hats came out, though, I had been playing the floor cymbal. Cats used to say "How can you play that hi-hat like that and keep time?" And I said, well, my teacher started me out with the floor cymbal and showed me how to do it.

You'd hear that after-beat going—"slap!" My only problem was that when the hi-hat came out, cats kept saying, "Beat on the hi-hat!"

V.W.: *When you actually first started playing, did you expect to be using your left foot as well?*

F.K.: No, I didn't know you had to use it for anything! My left foot was just sitting there idle.

V.W.: *Do you still go around listening to older drummers, James?*

J.B.: Yes, of course I do. You know sometimes your battery needs charging, and you have to plug into the main current again to get your vibes back up.

V.W.: *Do you think that this is a town where musicians respect each other? Do the younger ones respect the older?*

J.B.: I think so. I can't speak for too many other people, but I know where the music's coming from and I draw my experience from there. If it wasn't for them, I don't think I would be here. This would be a helluva world if there wasn't no music in it—just a world of voices and sounds. It'd be a bad dream, a nightmare.

V.W.: *What is the attitude of the cats who are younger than you towards traditional jazz?*

J.B.: From what I can gather, from students I've had, I guess it's just about the same. Everybody like to 'Second Line'. I don't know nobody here from New Orleans who don't like it and don't follow it. I don't care what kind of music they play, they all flock to the Second Line. And like the influence is still here; it never dies. I guess if all the older musicians die, the influence is still going to be carried on by the dudes who heard it. It may be altered a bit because of our way of hearing, but like the essence and the flavor will still be there.

V.W.: *What was this thing a couple of years ago when the Panthers wanted to break up the parades?*

J.B.: I guess it was a political, a racial sort of thing. To me, I guess they figured it was casting a bad image on black folks, but really, I see it as an expression of joy, an expression of celebration, of life. They're crazy—they'll never break up the Second Line.

F.K.: I'll tell you one thing about that Second Line—as long as there's New Orleans and a brass band, there will always be a Second Line. It's been going on since I was a kid, and it's still going on 59 years later.

J.B.: Right on! It's like an emotional experience, very uplifting—it really brings you out. It just infects you. There's something about a band in the streets . . .

F.K.: Yeah, I don't care what you're doing. You could be inside cooking a dinner, and somebody says there's a band coming down the street. And you say "Where?"

J.B.: All you got to hear is "boom, boom, b-boom"—"Where?" They'll never break it up.

V.W.: *Well, I understand the political aspect of it, but at the same time I see where things have changed and people are beginning to respect it, too.*

J.B.: True. Now I'm not acting out of disrespect, but this is part of our culture, this is part of our art. Alvin Battiste once said, "Way down deep from the depths of sorrow, music came." You know this came of that, back from slavery, and it was a sorry time. Now I wasn't there but from the history books I know they were—if I can use the expression—really being fucked over. But how could they possibly come up with a music that sounded like that? I guess it was there—nothing could stop it.

V.W.: *That's the whole thing. It seems to me that the music is a triumphant thing.*

J.B.: Right. It's like maybe you can capture the body, but you can't capture the spirit and the soul. No way.

V.W.: *Well, I think that's a very good note to end it on.*

J.B.: I have had a very good history lesson here today. Thank you, Freddy Kohlman, thank you very much.

"James Black, who died in New Orleans on 30 August at the age of 48, was a master drummer from a city that routinely produces percussion giants. That he boasts no entry in either Feather or the latest Grove is indicative of how the jazz world neglects those who don't play by the rules. Black preferred 'the Big Easy' after life in the fast lane, remaining an underground hero known only to locals and a circle of percussion cognoscenti." [1]

—Val Wilmer

Without a doubt, James Black was one of the key players in the New Orleans continuum. A multi-talented musician, Black played trumpet as a teenager, but by the end of high school was becoming known around town also as an accomplished drummer. Black was aware of and influenced by the older generation of New Orleans drummers, particularly Ed Blackwell, whose Gypsy Tea Room gig Black visited frequently. "When I heard Blackwell, he made me want to go home and practice," Black once said. "I didn't know you could play drums like that." [2]

By the late '50s, Black had absorbed all the major styles, from the cool west coast jazz of Shelly Manne to the sophisticated vocabularies of Art Blakey, Max Roach and "Philly" Joe Jones. These influences, combined with Black's own soulful southern feel, can be heard on Nat Adderley's *In the Bag,* an album of funky swing recorded in 1962.

Harold Battiste, president of AFO Records, recalls his impressions of Black during this period:

> *James, in spite of his youth, is probably the most aggressive and dynamic personality in the group. His playing reflects his personality very accurately. He is constantly bored with the present because the future is unexplored, and his mind is in the unexplored future . . . the present is already past.* [3]

Around the mid-sixties, Black's style began to change. According to David Lee, "James Black heard Elvin Jones and the next week he changed his whole drum style! Before that, he was more like a 'Philly' Joe Jones kind of drummer, really clean, straight-ahead and tight . . . You can hear it on those AFO records he did with Ellis Marsalis." [4]

Black moved to New York in 1964, where he played with Lionel Hampton, Cannonball Adderley, Yusef Lateef and Horace Silver before returning to New Orleans in the late '60s. Back home, Black resumed his musical association with Ellis Marsalis and once again became a dominating presence on the local modern jazz scene. With Marsalis, Black had an outlet for both his compositions and his dynamic playing. In an interview with Harold Battiste, Black describes their contribution to the New Orleans jazz scene:

> *We were keeping the music element of jazz— the art form of modern jazz—experimental jazz alive. We made Lu & Charlie's internationally known . . . that's right, me and Ellis.* [5]

In the '80s, Black recorded with Wynton and Branford Marsalis *(Fathers and Sons)* and on Ellis Marsalis' *Syndrome*. On both recordings, Black sounds more like a sideman rather than a star, but he still conveys a sense of musical depth. Black himself offered an explanation for the change:

> *I used to play very tense and right up on top of the beat and crowd everybody else out. Now I just relax, let the bass player find his spot, let the piano player find his spot. I just free everybody and let 'em go where they want to go instead of coming on the gig like most drummers and saying, "I play here, you play there."* [6]

Although Black was a highly respected jazz drummer, he crossed the line over to funk and R&B recording sessions for legendary producer, Allen Toussaint. In a December, 1982 interview with Scott Fish in *Modern Drummer*, Black also provides us with further insight into his multi-directional character and the unique sensibilities of a New Orleans musician.

> *I just wanted to be a jazz drummer and it became boring! After you see the same faces and play the same songs about 20,000 times, then what else is it? Man, there's got to be something else. I got off into funk and rock and went back to my roots. I thought, "I used to play rhythm and blues." That's true. I went back to that and found that that was paying off too. Now I get a chance to play a little R&B, a little rock, a little jazz, a little Afro-Cuban and a little of this and that. A little Martian music! Play some music from Pluto for a while; some of the avant-garde kind of stuff and just space out! Just get all your stuff out of you. Then after you play your little avant-garde for a while, go back and play some funk. If you can do that, you're well rounded.* [7]

On August 30, 1988, James Black died of a drug overdose. David Lee recalls how he heard the news:

George French called me up and said, "Well, you know, James is gone," and I said, "What? James who?" He said "James Black." I said "WHAT?!" I thought he was so wise, that he had been doing [drugs] so long, that . . . ain't nobody gonna take this cat out, he's streetwise, he knows what he's doing. And he OD'd, somebody gave him some wrong stuff. They brought him to [a local] hospital and when you OD on drugs you don't go to [this particular] hospital because they put you on a bed and put you in a hallway and leave you there. They don't stabilize you with life water or give you a shot to take you up or do something for you. They didn't do nothing, they just left him on the sheet til he died.[8]

Perhaps the most important legacy of James Black is his lasting influence on other New Orleans drummers, especially Herlin Riley. Compare Black's playing on Yusef Lateef's *Live at Pep's* with Riley's drumming with Wynton Marsalis and you will hear a remarkably similar interplay between the bass and snare drums of each, as well as a confidence— almost a cockiness—in the playing that is unmistakably James Black. Drummer Ernie Elly remembers Black as an inspiration in the truest sense:

Sometimes when I'd get down and out, you know, disgusted, I'd go check out the gig with James Black. He was a straight-ahead cat. A lot of cats didn't like him or were afraid of him, because he was so strong. Either you hated him or you loved him. I loved him. He had the fire . . . He had the New Orleans feeling, plus different polyrhythms, cross-rhythms, everything, he was phenomenal.[9]

SOURCES

1 Val Wilmer, *like listening to history*, Wire Magazine, London, April 1989

2 New Orleans Heritage, Jazz: 1956–1966, Interview with Harold Batiste, Accompanying booklet for box set (out of print).

3 ibid.

4 David Lee interview with Dan Thress, New Orleans, May 1994.

5 New Orleans Heritage, Jazz: 1956–1966, by Harold Batiste

6 *James Black: The Phone Always Rings*, by Val Wilmer, Melody Maker, August 11, 1973.

7 *Back Home with James Black*, by Scott Fish, *Modern Drummer* December, 1982

8 David Lee interview with Dan Thress, New Orleans, May 1994.

9 Ernie Elly interview with Dan Thress, New Orleans, May 1994.

James Black

JAMES BLACK SELECTED DISCOGRAPHY

Nat Adderley *In The Bag* (Original Jazz Classics); **Eric Gale** *A Touch Of Silk*; **Yusef Lateef** *Live at Pep's* (Impulse/GRP); **Wynton and Branford Marsalis** *Fathers and Sons* (Columbia); **Ellis Marsalis** *Syndrome* (Elm Records), *The Classic/Ellis Marsalis* (AFO Records); **Steve Masakowski** *Mars* (Nebula)

RECOMMENDED

JOSEPH "SMOKEY" JOHNSON

Smokey Johnson and Herlin Riley

Smokey Johnson is another drummer that you've mentioned as being very influential to your style. What type of ideas did you pick up from him?

Smokey had a tune out in the '60s, called "It Ain't My Fault." And on this tune, he would play the basic New Orleans drum pattern but on the hi-hat. And on the "and" of beat 4 he played on the floor tom.

CD TRACK 35

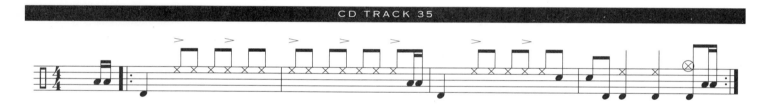

So he would play stuff like that. When he's playing straight-ahead, he knows how to slide the bass drum inside of the rhythms. For instance, he'll play stuff like this:

CD TRACK 36

Maybe that's a poor example of Smokey's playing, but that's how he influenced me. He really knows how to play the bass drum underneath the rhythms.

And there's a call-and-response between the snare drum and the bass drum.

Exactly.

With a steady ride going—

Cymbal keeps it going, the hi-hat is pretty much on 2 and 4, and there's a dialogue between the snare and the bass drum.

So I got a chance to hear all these different drummers and to check out how they played and how they approached the same music. And as a result of doing that, I've kind of taken some from James, a little bit from my uncle Popee, some from Smokey Johnson, from Ed Blackwell—and I've taken all those styles from these New Orleans drummers and kind of tried to formulate my own style with that language that they used.

HERLIN RILEY by Dan Thress

Live at the Village Vanguard, New York City

"Everything the band performed was propelled by the driving rhythm section of Reginald Veal on bass and Herlin Riley on drums, which kept shading all the grooves, suggesting shuffle rhythms or mambos, changing the character of the basic 4/4 swing. The two of them are air-tight, the bass and drums locking in with an authority and seamlessness that is only to be found in working groups."

—Peter Watrous, New York Times, *December, 1993*

For some New Yorkers Christmas came early that year, December 4, 1993 to be exact, when Wynton Marsalis's ensemble played a week-long stand at the legendary Village Vanguard. The second show Friday night was being recorded for Columbia Records; outside the club the line stretched down Seventh Avenue, while inside, every seat was taken, including those normally used by the band members, putting a few lucky fans practically onstage. This kind of intimacy with musicians is unquestionably the best way to experience jazz.

If there's not much of a stage at the Vanguard, there's no backstage at all: musicians hang out in a room that was part of the kitchen at one time and still contains a dishwasher.

To get to the stage from there, one has to work their way through the club, a routine that does away with the larger-than-life illusion created by television and big concert halls. Wynton and crew were high-spirited and loose as they took the stage, and the place began to feel like a private party.

Wynton told the audience, "We're here to swing." I thought that was a given, but I didn't know they would swing so deeply. The arrangements are compelling, musical, and very entertaining, with drummer Herlin Riley and bassist Reginald Veal anticipating and welcoming soloists, supporting in the tradition of the Blakey band. Picking up his tambourine, Herlin called the house to order

Herlin Riley at the Village Vanguard

for the first tune, "Uptown Ruler," drawn from New Orleans Mardi Gras Indian lore. The room tuned in as Herlin laid down a funky pattern in 5/4 with a New Orleans lope on the tambourine and bass drum, then began a roll call of Mardi Gras Indian chants that the rest of the band answered in chorus. As the singing and playing intensified, Herlin switched to sticks and brought in the horns.

Herlin plays his funky swing with an uncommon conviction that derives from his rich musical background. His comping figures, setups and fill-ins are like comments and opinions, clearly and directly stated, and his accompaniment always makes an astonishing, "why didn't I think of that" kind of sense.

Throughout the set, Herlin continued to pull out the unexpected. He started "A Long Way Home" with singing and chanting, accompanied by mallets on the snare and floor tom. Both his use of mallets and his loose latin and swing styles are reminiscent of Elvin Jones. Drummers sometimes get hung up on the cliches of jazz; this has never been Herlin Riley's downfall. His use of tambourine, floor tom, chanting, and his borrowing from styles such as second line have gained Herlin the respect of a wide range of drummers.

The phrase "musical journey" may be a little worn, but it really does apply to this version of Wynton's band. Their high-spirited version of Duke Ellington's "Rubber Bottom" transported the audience to New York in the 1940s, just as some of Wynton's recent compositions, drawing upon the harmonic and rhythmic beauty of the Spiritual church, evoked the deep South. Herlin's drums also resonate with the sounds of that church, and of the funky neighborhood bar, through the sophistication of a well-travelled musician. He follows in the tradition of many great jazz drummers who not only record but travel, bringing the music to those of us who need to see it as well as hear it.

To see Herlin Riley play is to gain an understanding of his musical attitude. His playing reflects a humble love and respect for the music. His playing is so heartfelt and personal that one is moved not only by the music, but by his soul, illumined in his proud face, as he tells you his musical story.

Wynton Marsalis

HERLIN RILEY SELECTED DISCOGRAPHY

Monty Alexander *Caribbean Circle* (Chesky); **Harry Connick, Jr.** (Columbia); **Ahmad Jamal** *Digital Works, Rossiter Road, Live At The Montreux Jazz Festival* (Atlantic); **Dr. John** *In A Sentimental Mood* (Warner Brothers); **Wynton Marsalis** *Standard Time: Volume 3–The Resolution Of Romance, The Majesty Of The Blues, Crescent City Christmas Card, Uptown Ruler, Levee Low Moan, Tune In Tomorrow, Citi Movement, In This House On This Morning, Peanuts* (Columbia); **Junko Onishi** *Live at the Village Vanguard* (Blue Note); **Marcus Roberts** *Deep In The Shed* (BMG), *Gershwin is For Lovers* (Novus); **David Torkanowsky** *Steppin' Out* (Rounder); **Steve Turre** *Sanctified Shells* (Antilles); **Bennie Wallace** *Bordertown* (Blue Note); **Michael White** *Crescent City Serenade* (Antilles); **Mark Whitfield** *Marksman* (Warner-Brothers).

Reflections and Observations on New Orleans Drummers

Bill Huntington has been a fixture on the music scene in New Orleans since the early '50s. He has performed and recorded with many of the greats of the modern era, and observed the playing of many more. Here he recounts, informally, his experiences with and memories of some of these important musicians.

1940s AND '50s

I guess we should start with *Paul Barbarin,* who was a major early drummer, composer and teacher. He led his own bands and recorded a lot, as did his brother Louis. He had a great press roll, a swinging feel and a good sense of form. I don't believe I ever got the chance to play with him, but I heard him play a lot in the fifties. *Abbie Brunies* was a member of another famous New Orleans musical family. He played in a strong, rhythmic, second line style, as did *Al Babin,* who played with Sharkey's Kings of Dixieland. I got to play with Abbie in the 1950s—there's a picture of me playing at his wedding in Al Rose's [and Edmond Souchon's] book, *New Orleans Jazz, A Family Album* (Louisiana State University Press). I understand that Abbie died on the bandstand. *Cié Frazier,* who I had the opportunity to record with in 1954, was a major influence and teacher. He had a strong beat, chops, and great ideas. And *Monk Hazel,* who played with Sharkey Bonano in the forties and fifties, was another great drummer.

Freddie Kohlman was with Sid Davda's band at the Mardi Gras lounge in the fifties. That was the first integrated band that I heard on Bourbon Street. I guess they pulled it off because it was Sid's club. I played with Freddie at Le Club, along with Ellis Marsalis and Lockjaw Davis. Freddie had just returned from Chicago, where he was the regular drummer at Jazz Ltd. He played strong and heavy, and was one of the first New Orleans drummers that I heard play different styles. I think he was a major influence on many of the younger drummers, including Shannon Powell and Herlin Riley.

I should also mention *Albert Jiles.* Albert was like a New Orleans version of Roy Haynes—very traditional, but he had all sorts of colorful ideas. He played a very funky street beat. I remember how, when you would go hear a parade in those days, umbrellas would be going up and down along with the beat the drummers were playing. Albert made a couple of records with an English trumpet player named Ken Colyer, and we did a record together called *Emile Barnes: Early Recordings* on the Folkways label.

Then there was a drummer I played with in George Lewis's band named *Joe Watkins.* He's on a lot of records under George's name. Joe Watkins wasn't a typical New Orleans drummer. He played a lot on the ride cymbal but for some reason, with that rhythm section, it really worked. That was an incredible rhythm section. He also had a happy, funky, personal thing. That's something I notice about the younger traditional drummers, even the ones from around here, it doesn't come off the same way. But of course, that's natural—you always play the music of your own era better.

I've always felt so comfortable playing with *Earl Palmer.* Earl's R&B playing is very different from his swing playing, and his swing playing is very much on top, whereas most New Orleans drummers play swing a little bit back. And *Joe Martin*—he was one of the lightest drummers I've played with, very sensitive, the first drummer I ever heard break up the cymbal patterns and play across the bar line. A bass player could walk in four or suspend the time. Joe was also a very good vibes player.

The contemporaries of Ed Blackwell were drummers like *Earl Cobble.* He was strongly influenced by Blackwell—of course, he was Blackwell's brother-in-law—but he played heavier, stronger time and Philly Joe-type solos. A lot of the guys I played with in the fifties and sixties had a little comping figure they would do with the left hand, like on the upbeat of beat two. I believe it came from Blackwell and it gave the time a lift—sort of a fifties hip-hop feel! *Happy Goldston,* who played with Papa Celestin, was, I believe, one of Blackwell's favorite drummers. He played on some records with Papa Celestin on the Bandwagon record label. I loved him, too. He had some very funky street beats. *Lou Timken* played in a pre-Blackwell style—a little stiff for me, but definitely one of the first modern players. Then there was *Kenny Ward, Lee Johnson* and *Lee Charleton*—I mention these drummers together because they all came from Bible Belt states and they were all strongly influenced by Blackwell. Kenny Ward I remember as being a strong, tasteful timekeeper. Same for Lee Johnson. Charleton was the leader of a great band in Biloxi, Mississippi, that included Don Reitan, a fine pianist; and a wonderful trumpet player, probably the best modern trumpet player to come out of New Orleans, Mike Serpas; and my bass teacher, Jay Cave. Lee Charleton also led the band that I played in with Serpas and Ellis Marsalis.

One guy I would like to mention who was really important as a teacher is *Lou Dilliard.* He taught Charlie Suhor and Reed Vaughan. *Charlie Suhor* was the most focused one of our little clique. He is one of the few people I know who loves jazz, regardless of race, style or era. He was influenced of course by Blackwell and had a dark sound, deep groove, good sense of form. Charlie was one of the best modern drummers of the fifties. And *Reed Vaughan* was like a child prodigy—he went out with Stan Kenton when he was 18 or 19. He played rather light and crisp; his influences at the time were New Orleans R&B, some of the street things, and the great drummers like Max Roach and Shelly Manne.

Getting into bebop, I used to play with *June Gardner* quite a bit. Once we did a trio gig at the Jazz and Heritage Festival with George Wein on piano.

June is one of the stalwarts of New Orleans bop drumming, with a strong, Jimmy Cobb-type feel on the ride cymbal. And I played a week-long trio gig with Ellis Marsalis and *Tony Bazely* at Le Club in the '60s. Tony Bazely was at his best playing strong bop drums. He spent some time in L.A., playing and recording with some great musicians.

1960s AND '70s
The main guy during this era, I'd have to say, was *James Black.* I used to play a lot with James before I left New Orleans in the sixties, and then again when I returned in the seventies. He had, for that time, some really unique polyrhythmic things happening, and the chops to pull them off. I remember once in the sixties when we were trading fours, he was taking these really "out" solos, and I could hear him softly counting out the ratio of his rhythms to the basic tempo. We did a record together with Ellis Marsalis called *Syndrome.*

James was quite a character. He kind of had a school of his own. I didn't see that much of a relationship between James and Boogie [Ed Blackwell]. James was a heavier drummer and his beat was different. Blackwell's beat was lighter and more buoyant. I think James Black was a big influence on Herlin Riley, Ernie Elly, and a lot of the younger drummers in the seventies and eighties such as *Bobby Breaux,* who's a great drummer and lives in Dallas now. He's got some interesting stories about taking lessons from James!

I think *David Lee* is one of the best New Orleans modernists. David plays strong but with that buoyant, dancing cymbal beat, a good sense of form and a deep groove. I've played club dates with him and he plays all styles well. I think he sounds great on *A Night at Snug Harbor* with Ellis Marsalis.

I should definitely mention *Jimmy Zitano* from Boston, who was with Al Hirt in the sixties. Jimmy stayed in New Orleans for quite a few years. I just got a call from a friend of mine in Dallas who read an article about Jimmy—he died while he was playing drums. He died right after taking a

solo. Jimmy was a really unique cat. He influenced a lot of drummers, including Tony Williams.

And I heard *John Boudreaux* play jazz on Bourbon Street with tenor saxophonist Charlie Farlie. I thought he was very influenced by Blackwell.

1970s AND '80s
Herlin Riley was in the Al Hirt band with me—I got him on that gig. When he came in he just lifted that band up and made it into something else! He must have been around 26 years old when he joined. He *made* that gig. I don't think Al Hirt ever sounded better. He needed a rhythm section like that. After that, Herlin went with Ahmad Jamal and then with Wynton Marsalis. I also played with *Freddie Staehle* in the Al Hirt band, in the early sixties. He had an influence on many of the younger drummers. I understand that he's playing great with Dr. John. He had an older brother, *Paul Staehle,* who was also a fine drummer.

I played quite a bit with *Bob French* and his band—Bob is another one who plays very strong and can really swing. He's evidently considered a traditional drummer now.

Ernie Elly is an excellent modern drummer who is equally comfortable playing traditional. We played together on a couple of Doc Cheatham records. He has a funky feel, nice cymbal beat, and a good sense of form.

Johnny Vidacovich has what I call a "vocal" style of playing the drums, he plays tunes on the drums. I hear Blackwell's influence on Johnny's playing, but I think he got Blackwell through David Lee. Johnny and I have played a lot together since the '70s. He's one of the most sensitive and intelligent players—on any instrument— that I have ever worked with. I think *Ricky Sebastian* was influenced by Johnny, but I see a closer relationship to James Black, in the cross-rhythms that he plays as well as his sound. James had really crisp chops and would put accents in different places, same as Ricky does.

Another great drummer around here

is *Bunchy Johnson,* who plays with George French's band. Bunchie was Allen Toussaint's favorite session drummer for a long time. He's a very popular drummer, and one of the nicest cats you will ever meet. He's a contemporary of Johnny Vidacovich, but more in the Smokey Johnson/Zig Modeliste funk type school. *Smokey Johnson* is really a definitive New Orleans drummer. He was one of the first guys to incorporate street beats into commercial R&B. I think James Black was influenced by Smokey, more so than by Blackwell. There's something tighter in the beat, and to me, Smokey plays like that. He's a great drummer.

I don't get much of a chance to play with *Shannon Powell,* but I dig him. He and Herlin are both strong, aggressive drummers with great chops—they can play all the styles. Shannon is best known for his work with Harry Connick, Jr.

Finally, there's a wave of new drummers that should be mentioned, such as *Brian Blade, Jason Marsalis, Adonis Rose* and *Julian Garcia.* These are the people to watch now who are continuing the New Orleans drumming tradition.

Bill Huntington

"I want the rhythm to have a little bit more of a curve to it,
rather than just coming straight at you."

—Johnny Vidacovich

STREET BEATS: MODERN APPLICATIONS

Johnny Vidacovich *(va-DOCK-a-vich)*

"I had a great teacher between the ages of 12 and 17, and his name was Charles Suhor. He made sure that I knew all kind of dixieland beats to play, because I was playing in dixieland bands when I was about 13 years old—a group of all kids. And, he taught me lots of good solid dixieland approaches, for keeping the time happening and for playing different fills and so on. When I was around 14 years old, he introduced me to the music of Charlie Parker and drummer Shadow Wilson. So I started to listen to Bird and Dizzy and be-bop drummers like Shadow Wilson and Max Roach. And I really didn't know what I was listening to, it was way over my head, but he would say 'Learn how to play this.' So I did. Anything he would tell me to learn, I would learn."

D.T.: *When anybody mentions New Orleans drummers, your name always comes up. I think that has a lot to do with your versatility. We can hear you playing on R&B as well as jazz records, and I'd like to cover those different styles if we can. As a starting point, can we begin with the "street beats," or "second line" feels that you're known for.*

J.V.: Well, I'll play a street beat, and it will focus on a rhythm, like a clave, that I will improvise around. And the clave is a real simple one:

3:2 son clave

You know, a simple standard clave, except that it's a more marching-type thing and a looser feel, but that's basically the skeleton of the rhythm. Let me just play a little bit of that and improvise off it.

One thing I notice is that your sticks are moving around and getting different nuances out of the drum.

Well, I learned this as a kid watching the old guys play. Basically, they used the snare drum in three parts: the center for an exact attack; then about halfway from the middle, you get more of a sustained sound, and then towards the edge, you get a ring. So if you take a simple rhythm like this:

"BUZZIN' & DRAGGIN'"

I'm playing it all in the center, but for it to sound more legato and more melodic, I move the sticks out and start to buzz it a little bit toward the edge of the drum and the other two sections of the drum. Let me play that same beat with a few drags, and when I say the word "drag," I mean actually buzzing the stick, literally dragging it. My hands are going in and out so it will be smoother, because if I played it all in the center, it would all sound very *ticky-ticky*. I want it to sound more like: *zaadodo zaadodo*. So here's the same pattern using the different sections of the drum.

I'm kind of moving from the center of the drum towards the rim and then out a little bit to get the ring. Then I've got time happening with my right hand. So I'm using the drum to get around, rather than hitting it all in the same place at the same time. I want the rhythm to have a little bit more of a curve to it, rather than just coming straight at you.

Could you demonstrate going back and forth between a swing feel and a second line feel on the snare drum?

Sure, here we go:

CD TRACK 42

Second line

L on HH

R on drums

Swing

Second line

R R L R R LL R   LLL R R L R R LL R   R R L R R LL R   LLL R LLL R LLL R

"Carnival"

DRUMS

A Melody

B

C

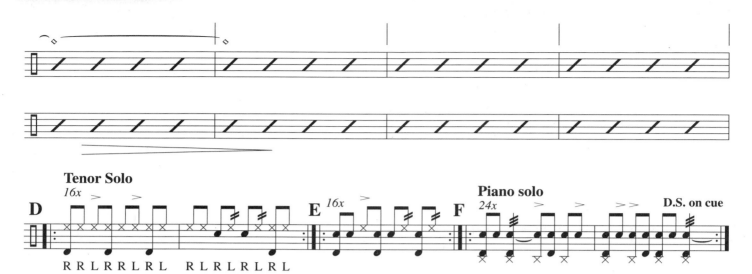

Tenor Solo

16x

D

R R L R R L R L   R L R L R L R L

E *16x*

Piano solo

F *24x*

D.S. on cue

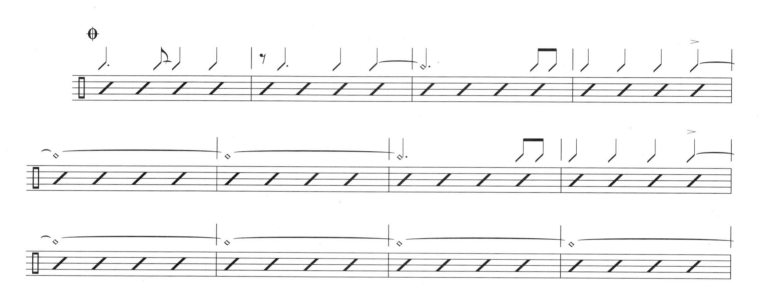

vamp fade

SYNCOPATION EXERCISES

One of the other things that's really unique about New Orleans drumming is all the syncopated figures. You've told me that you have some exercises that can help drummers get this together. Could you demonstrate some of these exercises?

OK. I have two syncopation exercises that I use for students. One's good for a jazz (triplet) feel, and the other one is good for funk because it deals with straight eighth-notes. The idea is to have the right hand play straight time and with your other limbs, you improvise using upbeats. Here's an example with the right hand playing time (quarter-notes) and upbeats on the bass drum and snare drum:

CD TRACK 44

Now here's the basic beat:

CD TRACK 45

Now make use of some of those upbeats by adding them to places where they normally wouldn't be.

CD TRACK 46

"If you practice this exercise over and over, and you start to play jazzier things, you will find yourself using more upbeats, which will create syncopation. And syncopation in funk as well as jazz is what really intrigues the listener."

Now to loosen up with triplets. Most drummers have a habit of always playing on the downbeat when they're playing a jazz ride pattern. For example, if someone counts off a tune: 1, 2—1, 2, 3, 4—they always hit that "1" that follows. To get your limbs away from automatically hitting on downbeats, and to create more of a syncopated feeling, take a triplet and break the triplet up amongst your different limbs. For example, the right hand plays quarter-notes, and you subdivide in triplets: 1-2-3, 1-2-3, 1-2-3, 1-2-3, [1 trip-let, 2 trip-let, 3 trip-let, 4 trip-let]. And with that, I play the snare drum on "2," the bass drum on "3." And then reverse that: the bass drum on "2," the snare drum on "3." The hi-hat on "2," the snare drum on "3." And all the variations. So it sounds like this:

CD TRACK 47

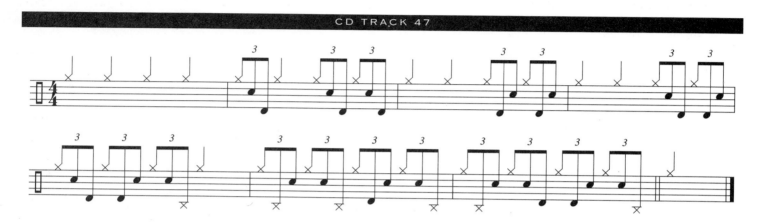

In this exercise, the bass drum and snare drum never hit on "1." [Oops, in the following example I played my bass drum on beat 1 —J.V.] If you practice this exercise over and over, and you start to play jazzier things, you will find yourself using more upbeats, which will create syncopation. And syncopation in funk as well as jazz is what really intrigues the listener. You know, because we normally feel things, **strong**–weak, **strong**–weak, **strong**–weak. So when you start playing this—

CD TRACK 48

Swing feel

—you're getting in between all the beats, and the syncopation you are creating is what really makes the listener feel "dance-y." To control syncopation and use it in different places is really what gets the listener to move, because you're avoiding naturally strong beats by using anticipations (the upbeats).

"You have to remember, priority number one with the drums is to keep the time happening. So just play that time accurately with your right hand, like a metronome, and then all the syncopation comes from the other three limbs of your body.

It's sort of like paddling a boat in the water and you have a nice steady rhythm going—I'm in the back of the boat and you're in the front of the boat with your back to me—and I put my hands on the side of the boat and give the boat a good shake. You're in the front and you really think you're going to fall over, but I know in reality that I have control of the boat. So the feeling that you have up front, not seeing me from behind shift the rhythm of the boat like that, is syncopation. And you get real excited in the front, because I messed with the rhythm. If you're playing funk, it would be the same thing:

CD TRACK 49

WEAK BEATS

You know, messin' around—rockin.' For me, it involves putting emphasis on the weak beats like, the "and" of beat 4. Beat 4 is a weak beat and it's also quite emphasized in the music around here. Even in the old days they emphasized beat 4, usually of a two-measure pattern:

BEAT 4

The emphasis on beat 4, the weakest beat, comes right before the strongest beat, beat 1. The listener gets ready for that "1" to come, but you put a big emphasis on the beat right before that, he can feel it in his body, physically speaking, because you're shifting the molecules around from a regular "boom-chick boom-chick"—creating a danceable-type feeling.

When you're playing your syncopated exercises, your right hand is usually playing a straight pattern so everything else can be offset against it, right?

Exactly. You have to remember, priority number one with the drums is to keep the time happening. So just play that time accurately with your right hand, like a metronome, and then all the syncopation comes from the other three limbs of your body.

PROFESSOR LONGHAIR

"HER MIND IS GONE"

"'Fess wanted everything with an edge. Funk with an edge. He didn't want it to lay back into that blue-grey situation. He always wanted me to push it just a little harder. If you listen to Crawfish Fiesta, you'll hear a lot of tunes that are very snap, crackle, and pop, but they're also greasy."

—Johnny Vidacovich
Modern Drummer
October, 1990

John, let's talk about your playing with Professor Longhair. You played on his classic record Crawfish Fiesta. *You sound great on that record. Let's go over "Her Mind is Gone." What's the basic beat on that?*

OK, the basic beat is like one of those kind of old rock 'n' roll beats, you remember this kind of beat:

So for that tune, I keep that beat happening and I put some ornamentation on it. My right hand is always going to keep that time in eighth-notes, and my left hand is always going to drag the fourth beat. The basic beat is still always going to be there. A little syncopation on the bass drum, but not much.

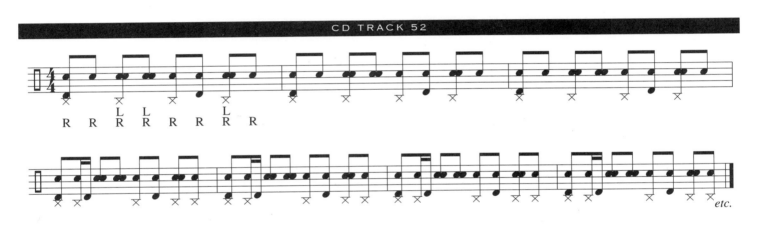

Now with ornamentation, using some drags with the left hand and sixteenth-notes with the right hand, but staying with the same beat, or clave, whatever you want to call it.

Her Mind is Gone

"Her Mind is Gone" main groove

CD TRACK 54

DRUMS

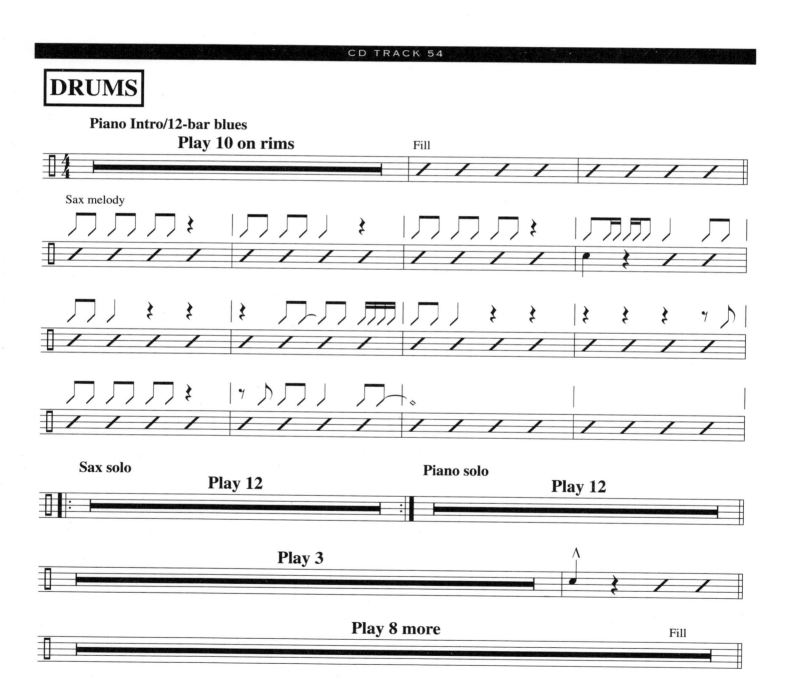

Sax melody

Tag

Fine

So the left hand drags first, the right follows, and then you move them around the drum to get the different sound sources.

Exactly, I let the drum sing. I want to use as much of the drum for variations as I can. I want the drum to sing continuously, and the way to make it sing continuously, rather than having each beat stick out, is play in the parts of the drum where it rings and buzzes a little bit to make it sound more legato. Remember how in old swing music the guys used to play time with a roll:

CD TRACK 55

Playing this style is not too different from the old swing styles, because they used a lot of presses and drags on different parts of the drum to keep it buzzing—to keep the sound continuous. I do the same thing so it won't sound so military. I try to use a lot of looseness.

Do you think of a pre-determined number of bounces, or are you just going for the sound?

I'm going by the motion of my arms to keep the original beat going, and when I get to the drags, I let the stick and the drum work it out together. I just drop the stick on the drum and control the bounces—when to take them away and when to let them go down. And basically I rely on the sound of the instrument to make it sound as smooth and legato as possible.

"BIG CHIEF"

Let's go over another Professor Longhair groove: "Big Chief."

I learned the beat from listening to it on jukeboxes. Again, all the syncopation here is with the left hand. The right hand plays straight eighth-notes, and the bass drum plays "4 + 1." I play the eighth-notes with my right hand on the side of the floor tom—on the shell. I don't know what it looks like written down, I just learned it by ear.

And with the left hand I play the syncopation right before every one of those beats and it really gives it a crazy syncopated feel.

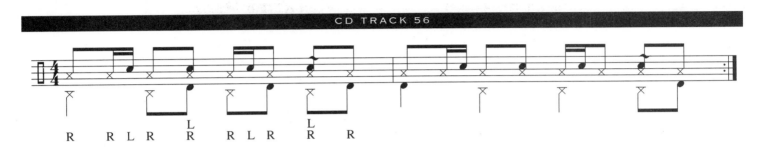

CD TRACK 56

"I was looking for something [unique] to play on a record. I turned the floor tom over on its side and I played on the side of the floor tom [right hand] and I was playin' rim-shots on the snare drum. I also took two sticks full of Coke caps that I had nailed on. I had two big ones that I overdubbed on that track. They used to let me do almost whatever I wanted to do on the session. That was a good session. That was the best thing that Professor Longhair ever did. That's Earl King singin' and whistlin."

—Smokey Johnson, drummer on the original "Big Chief" session

"Big Chief"

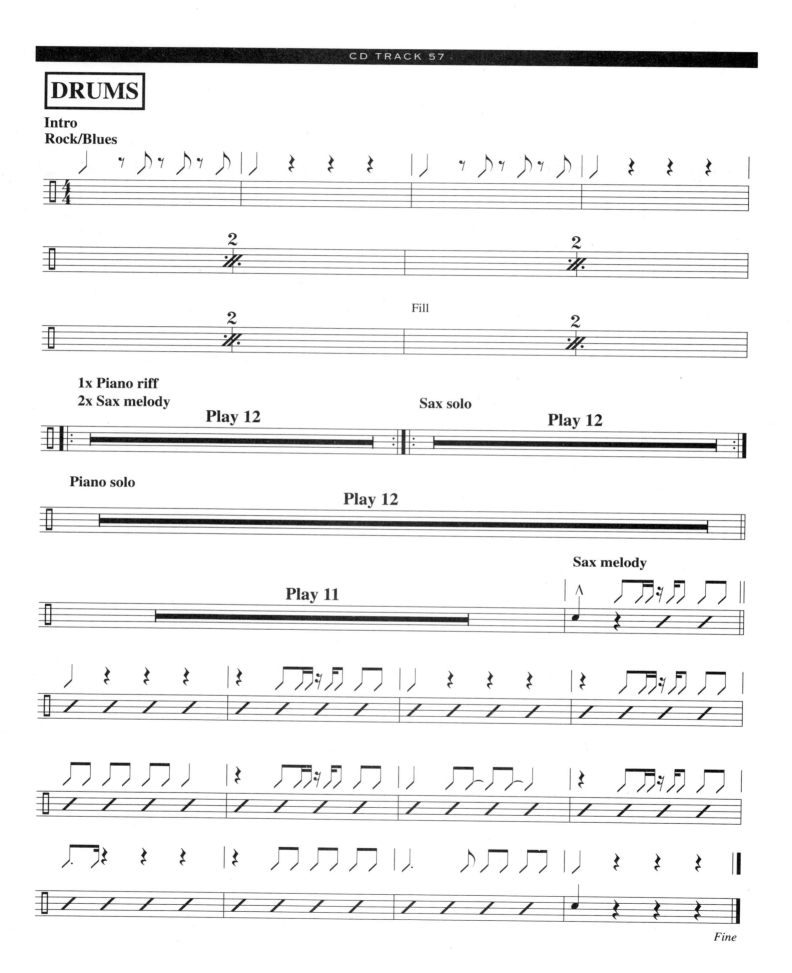

Fine

With that beat, you have two reference points: the straight eighth-notes with your right hand, and the quarter-notes on your hi-hat.

You play quarter-notes with the hi-hat and it works out fine. That's the beat I heard on the record all my life and I learned it as a kid. It's sort of a clave. The latin influence is dominant in all of these beats. A lot of times in some of the funk beats around here, too, you find the reverse clave [2:3 son clave]. Zigaboo [Modeliste, legendary drummer with the Meters] does that a lot, he'll use that clave beat in a tune like "Workin' In A Coal Mine."

CD TRACK 58

Then again, we still emphasize that fourth beat. That's always going to be characteristic—pretty much always, that emphasis on "4."

So many of the beats and rhythms that you play draw on other traditions from the city.

Absolutely. You can definitely tell the African and the Cuban influence in all of the beats.

This "no frills straight ahead R&B record" by New Orleans blues singer Roland Stone features Johnny's great southern, unaffected grooves.

Orleans Records

JOSEPH "SMOKEY" JOHNSON

From Sugarboy to the Fatman

I was raised in the sixth ward, where all the happenings were at.

—*Smokey Johnson*

A lot of good drummers come from that neighborhood—you, James Black—what about John Boudreaux?

Yeah, he was from the sixth ward. They have little-bitty kids in that neighborhood playing instruments. You heard about Trombone Shorty? He's going to be a good one.

Do you play another instrument?

Trombone was my first instrument.

When did you start playing the drums?

When I was around 12. I played trombone first. We had to to play two instruments. James Black and I had the same teacher, Yvonne Bush. She used to live next door to me on St. Peters and I took lessons from her before she started teaching school. She taught a lot of us.

Everybody talks about your versatility as a drummer. You play R&B and jazz with equal authority.

Well, most of the cats around here that were playing when I was coming up played both jazz and rock or whatever you want to call it.

Who were some of the drummers who influenced you?

I used to listen to cats like Ed Blackwell.

In clubs?

Yeah, in clubs, he used to let me sit in.

How old were you?

I must have been 18 or 19.

Was anyone else sitting in on Blackwell's gigs at that time?

Well, John Boudreaux, but that was about it.

What is Boudreaux's playing like?

He's a good drummer. A jazz drummer, too. He used to play with the Hawkettes, who became the Neville Brothers.

Was Idris Muhammad (Leo Morris) playing around town then?

Yeah, he was playing with the Neville Brothers, but they had a different name.

Who else influenced you besides Blackwell?

Wilber Hogan and Charles "Honeyboy" Otis.

What about Earl Palmer?

I used to listen to Earl a lot.

Playing jazz?

No, he was doing a lot of studio work. He could play!

What about "Hungry"?

Charles Williams? He was a good player. He played R&B.

So as far as your jazz influences, they would be Wilber Hogan, Honeyboy and Blackwell, with Blackwell being the main one.

Yeah, 'cause I used to see him more than the other cats.

And your R&B influences were Hungry, Earl and Honeyboy. Anyone else?

A fellow named Eugene Jones—we used to listen at each other. Me and John Boudreaux used to practice together. We all came up together. We were like, 12, 13, 14 years old.

David Lee also told me about playing with other drummers.

We used to practice eight hours a day, every day! And then one day you just wake up and you're playing. That's the way it goes. You've got to practice. Before you know it, you'll be playing something.

When did you get your first set of drums?

My first year in high school, that's when I got my own set. Before that I played the school's drums.

What was the first group you played with?

"Sugarboy" (James Crawford) and the Cha-Paka-Shaweez. I played with them for a long time.

What was the first record that you made?

The first big thing I played on was an album called New Orleans House Party with Dave Bartholomew. After I did that, I started recording with everybody.

Everybody heard it on the jukeboxes and wanted to know who that drummer was!

I played with everybody after that.

How old were you?

Around 19.

On New Orleans House Party, *what drums were you using?*

I was using my own drums, Slingerland, with a 22" bass drum.

With padding for a nice, deep, funky tone?

Yeah.

And what kind of snare drum?

Slingerland—chrome.

And the toms?

Three toms. It was a black set. Slingerland made some good drums.

Two cymbals?

I had a lot of cymbals. Blackwell gave me a cymbal, a couple of other cats gave me cymbals. Cymbals were high [priced]. And if I didn't have my own, I would borrow John Boudreaux's.

Were you doing a lot of playing in clubs then?

Oh yeah! I was 17 years old and I was playing at the Dew Drop.

What was a typical playing week like?

When I was in my early twenties, I used to play in a place across the river from Baton Rouge called Port Allen. I played there six nights a week with Sugarboy. We used to stay all week in Baton Rouge and come home on Sunday night and head straight to the Dew Drop.

Who did you work with at the Dew Drop?

I played with a cat named Gus Fountana who was in Guitar Slim's band. He quit and formed his own band at the Dew Drop. Allen Toussaint was in that band.

Were any recordings made of that band?

No, uh-uh.

Who was the next big artist that you worked with after Sugarboy?

Earl King. We'd play around town and in Baton Rouge.

Were you doing any jazz gigs at this time (the early 60s)?

Yeah, I was doing jazz, but there wasn't many jazz gigs around. We used to get together and go jam at the union hall.

Was Ellis Marsalis part of these sessions?

No. "Mouse" Bonati, George French, Earl Turbinton, Fred Kemp. It was alright during this time, but there wasn't too many jazz joints to play in. I made all my money playing with Sugarboy.

What would you make on a typical night with Sugarboy?

We were working by the week, we used to make around $300 a week. That was a lot of money back then.

　　After I left Sugarboy, I started playing jazz with Red Tyler. I was scared to go on that gig. That's where I really learned how to play. I learned a lot of tunes, 'cause Red doesn't play a lot of the regular tunes that other guys play.

That seems to be another New Orleans trait, learning tunes instead of just beats or licks. When did you move to Detroit and begin working for Motown?

It was in the '60s. Me and Earl King and a bunch of us went up there with Joe Jones. I could have stayed there as long as I wanted.

Joseph "Smokey" Johnson

What was the scene like?

I would record all day, from 9 to 5. Then I had a gig about three nights a week.

Playing R&B?

We used to play everything. I had the gig as long as I wanted. But if I had a recording date in the evening, then we wouldn't play the gig.

Were you making decent money with Motown?

Yeah, I was making good money. The money was alright.

Did you know which artists you were recording with at the time?

A lot of those sessions were just tracks. We did tracks all day long.

Who was playing bass with you on these sessions?

Well, there wasn't just one regular bass player.

Were there other drummers also working for Motown?

When I went there, they had been using two drummers on a recording date. After I got there, they only used me.

They didn't need two drummers anymore!

Those drummers up there didn't play much bass drum. A drummer from around here plays the full set.

Herlin Riley: I think that it is the feeling and the placement of your bass drum within the music. It's not the technique or playing a lot of notes, it's more about knowing when and where to drop it.

Herlin, when did you first hear Smokey?

Well, Smokey and my uncle Popee were really good friends. When I was growing up they used to have rehearsals at my house.

Were the Meters an extension of the type of music you had been recording?

Oh, those songs that they were doin'? Yeah. Just after I started putting those tunes out, they did "Sissy Strut."

They saw you could have an instrumental hit.

Yeah. I might put out something else; I have a lot of tunes.

Was Zig a real "student" of yours?

(laughs) Zig knows all my old tricks. I used to have a tooth chipped off, and I later saw Zig with his tooth chipped. Zig used to talk like me. We were tight. Zig is a good drummer. But he's not a jazz drummer, he doesn't play jazz.

What happened to James Black after he came back to New Orleans from New York? Was his playing strong?

A lot of cats wouldn't hire James. He died when I was in Berlin. I kind of figured something like that was going to happen. He was a good drummer, though. New Orleans is a drummer's town; always has been.

Why is that?

Well, New Orleans swing music—or Dixieland, as the old men call it—New Orleans swing music has a beat. And you don't hear that beat being played anywhere

Smokey Johnson

else. And it kind of rubs off on drummers when they're young. I can be playing a tune like "Cherokee," or "Giant Steps" at a fast tempo, and I can break it down in the chorus by changing rhythms. I can play some second line for eight bars. So you can hear that type of New Orleans swing music in a lot of the jazz drummers around here. I think that's where New Orleans drummers get their beat from.

You can hear it in rock, too. I can play with (bassist) George French and he'll be playing the same thing on his bass that I'm playing on my bass drum, with no rehearsal. It just comes out that way. It doesn't seem like it should come out that way, but it does.

What kind of cymbals were you using when you played with Fats Domino?
Sabian.

Were you using a Chinese cymbal?
No, I like to use that when I'm playing Dixieland.

Do you have to have that cymbal to play Dixieland?
Yeah, you got to have it. Freddie Kohlman showed me how to use that cymbal. A whole lot of people don't know how to use it. They hit it. You don't hit it—you brush it with the stick on the edge where the rivets are. People also play the regular jazz ride pattern on it, and it doesn't sound right. I play that cymbal behind trombone solos.

And you play just enough half-notes on the cymbal to get a light roar going.
Yeah, but you don't attack it. Freddie Kohlman was great at it.

Do you play traditional grip?
I don't play that other grip.

Did you ever work another job to support yourself and your family?
No, I've never had a job other than playing music. I know a lot of cats who had to do it. But I always had a gig.

How big is your family?
Well, I've been married twice and I've raised two families and never had to have a day job.

What was it like working with Fats Domino?
I started with Fats in 1973. I had been playing with Dave Batholomew working for Imperial. With Fats we always traveled right. We stayed in the best hotels, and we all had our own rooms.

JOHNNY VIDACOVICH ON SMOKEY JOHNSON

I distinctly remember going to see Smokey when I was 14 years old. He used to play at this place called Germania Hall. So this was a white establishment, run by some guys from the VFW or something, that would have these weekly functions where all the teenagers could go for a quarter. And nine out of ten times it would be a black band, and Smokey played with fifty percent of those bands. It would be a regular thing for me. Friday night came along and boom! Twenty-five cents and I'd go hear Smokey for three hours. It was all R&B, soul stuff.

Did you hear him play jazz?
Those particular bands would usually play three jazz tunes, which amounted to about twenty minutes, and then the singer would come out and they would do rock and funk tunes for an hour. Jazz was mostly in bars, so at that young age I couldn't go hear it. But when I was 15 or 16 I used to go and stand outside bars to hear jazz.

Was the Dew Drop Inn still going at this time?
Yeah, but I didn't go in that neighborhood. That was strictly a black neighborhood, and in the early 1960s a white teenager couldn't go there.

Did you hear Smokey with Sugarboy?
I can't remember. He used to play with bands that backed up singers, like Ernie K-Doe and Eddie Bo. It was like a show. He would always be the drummer—well, not always, but he was the guy that I looked for. I'd spend that quarter and not move for three hours. I'd buy a couple of cokes and end up getting a three-hour music lesson for less than a dollar.

June Gardner, Stanley Stephens, Smokey Johnson.

"OPEN SHUFFLE" FEEL

Can you describe that feel of the Red Tyler composition, "New Orleans Cakewalk?"

It's an "open shuffle"—somewhere between a straight rhythm and a shuffle rhythm. And for me, the way I get that in-between-ness is to focus on the upbeats again. If you focus a little bit on the upbeat, when you put the emphasis on it, it's so close to the downbeat that it lags into the downbeat. So let me try to play it. This is what it would be like straight:

CD TRACK 59

Straight

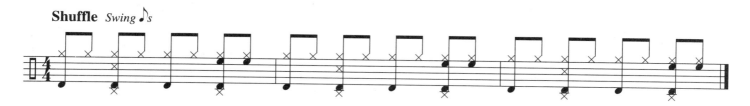

And this is what it would be like as a shuffle:

CD TRACK 60

Shuffle *Swing ♪s*

Now I've got to get somewhere in between that, so just let me mess around here for a second and see if I can get it.

CD TRACK 61

Swing ♪s

"New Orleans Cakewalk"

"New Orleans Cakewalk" main groove

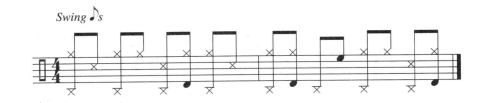

CD TRACK 62

Always keep triplets in mind, just to make sure it stays a little loose and not too straight. You have to come up with your own little things that work for you to loosen it up.

And the fills that you play can go either way: straight eighth-notes or triplets.

Exactly, because it's so open. I'm always feeling a triplet or hearing a triplet somewhere, to keep me from straying too far to the straight side of the eighth-note. Sometimes in my pattern I play:

CD TRACK 63

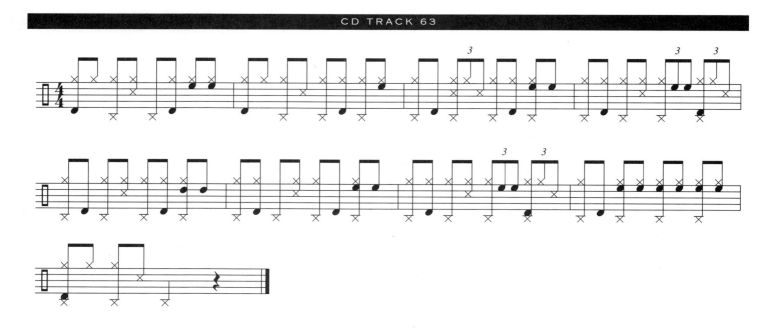

TENSION & RELEASE

But sometimes when you bring out the straight eighth-notes at the right time, it can create a little tension and release, just like the harmonic motion of the "New Orleans Cakewalk." It has really pretty harmonies, and if you put those straight eighth-notes in certain places, it kind of lifts the tune up into the next change.

I really try to feel both grooves at the same time, and be able to go into either groove, the straight groove or the triplet groove. That's why I can't stress enough about learning how to manipulate and use upbeats—syncopated beats. If you do these exercises for twenty minutes a day, eventually they will start seeping in and become part of you. So it's important to have the control and ability to rock the boat without making it capsize. The more the boat rocks, the more fun it is. But it's not fun to flip over.

Let's talk about your jazz influences. Who were some of the drummers who were influential in developing your style?

Around town, it was definitely James Black and David Lee. They both had the ability to play funk as well as jazz, and I used to go to different places as a teenager and listen to them play. They were also able to incorporate a "street" approach to playing the drums, because they're from here. I think when I was young, I really realized the relationship between marching street-type snare drumming and applying that to jazz or rock, funk, or whatever. I could hear those elements in their playing. They were two of my main jazz influences, as well as influencing my approach to playing on the snare drum.

I learned a lot of things about composition from James Black. He was real good at playing a tune as a composition, and I found the parts he would play to be quite meaningful. He was using the different timbres of the set and approaching it like a small orchestra. The drums have the ability to be very soft and very loud, and you should take advantage of the extreme range that can be played on the instrument. That definitely comes into play in jazz, because you have to play softly and delicately—

As well as using mallets and brushes.

Absolutely.

I always listened to Zig, he's maybe a year or two older than me and he was always playing around town, we were always crossing paths. I listened to David Lee a lot when I was between 16 and 21. He used to play with George Davis, Willie Tee, and Earl Turbinton. He later went to New York and recorded with Dizzy Gillespie and Sonny Rollins.

I listened to Ernie Elly a lot, he's still playin' around here. A lot of guys left New Orleans, but many of them stayed and would resurface after 10 or 15 years and start making an impact again, like Ernie Elly.

What does he sound like?

Loose. He's right-handed and left-footed—real loose. He's got that military thing but it's a loose New Orleans sound—smooth and legato.

I listened to Smokey Johnson, he was a great early R&B session player and was on a lot of the hits. He's still around, playing with Fats Domino and some of the other guys. As a kid, I could hear a lot of these guys for very little money. You could hear Smokey Johnson playing with Ernie K-Doe or Benny Spellman at these kid dances for 25 or 50 cents.

Another big influence during this time was Freddie Staehle, who recorded with Dr. John. He spent some time in L.A. I used to listen to him a lot.

There was a guy named Jack Sperling who used to play with Al Hirt and Pete Fountain. I saw him a little bit when I was a youngster. He had really good rudimental chops, and he could fit that "street" thing very well into Dixieland. He had really nice facility, and because he was an older man, he really knew how to make rolls swing. He could play time with just playing rolls on the snare drum.

So as a youngster, I had exposure not just to what was on the radio, but by playing Dixieland I got to meet a lot of older guys, and they gave me a lot of things to work on and refine.

So you took their advice and combined it with your own playing experiences.
Yes, absolutely.

And you didn't turn down any gigs?
Never turned down a gig.

You didn't say, "I'm going to be a jazz player," or "I'm going to be an R&B player"—
No. I couldn't do that. I just tried to play everything that was thrown at me, and I honestly feel that, unless you've got a lot of money, you've got to be ready! You've got to be ready when the phone rings to play the gig, you know? Unless somebody's supporting you. I just believe that music is music, it's the way you play it. It's your attitude when you're playing it.

When I'm playing, man, I draw from everything that I've learned—Dixieland stuff, funny stuff. I'm always applying these street claves to everything that I play. Because it's so innate. When it comes to playing be-bop, I strongly relate it to my Dixieland roots.

I also hear the more modern "open" influences of drummers like Paul Motian and Jon Christensen in your playing.

Well, Paul Motian is absolutely my favorite drummer. When it comes to listening to drummers, I love to listen to Paul Motian. There's something about his time, he's so unaffected by excitement and things, he's just so focused. He plays lots of little phrases and contour melody-type ideas on the drums. I remember when I first heard Paul Motian was on *The Village Vanguard Sessions,* with Bill Evans on piano and Scott LaFaro on bass.

For the first nine months I listened to it, I thought, "I love this music, when the bass player's not walking, he's playing free counterpoint"—and months went by before I even realized: who's the drummer? What's the drummer playing? It was so subtle that it took me a long time, as a youngster, to really even want to listen to the drums. And then I said, "Wow, all of this music's going on and he's right there!" You know? He really created a beautiful cushion—a sheet of rhythm—for Scott LaFaro and Bill Evans to play over—all of that counterpoint.

In the way he broke up the cymbal rhythm, he reminded me a lot of Kenny Clark. I really like Paul Motian. I've learned a lot from him. And of course I had to stay tuned with guys like Tony Williams, you've just got to. I mean, he's so happening, you've got to be aware of it.

Ernie Elly

DAVID LEE by Dan Thress

Evolution

David Lee, to me, was the much more refined of the bunch when it came to playing. Smokey and Zig were very raw: David and James Black composed at the drumset. David set me off in that whole direction of linear playing when I was really young and didn't even know what I was doing.

—Johnny Vidacovich

"I was born uptown, in the 12th or 13th ward, between Marengo and Coliseum. Every Mardi Gras, my mother would take us with our masks and we would go to the parade. I remember hearing the man play the bass drum and every time he hit that bass drum it was going in my stomach. It was like he was hitting me, you know? And I said, 'Yeah, that's what I want to do, I want to play the drums!' I must have been about five or six years old."

—David Lee

David Lee was born January 4, 1941 and got his first drum, a Ludwig junior-sized field drum, at the age of twelve, after years of demonstrating his enthusiasm for drumming on his family's telephone books. At fifteen, he told his father that, with a full drumset, he could be working within a week; his father supplied the downpayment, and David promptly got a gig.

> Solomon Spencer, who was a band director at Walter J. Korn high school, took me, Earl Turbinton, Willie Tee, Aaron Neville and I think Leo Morris [Idris Muhammad] and he would get us little gigs at frat houses where we made eight, ten dollars apiece a night. We played all the Little Richard and Fats Domino kind of songs for the frat people.

Like many other New Orleans drummers, Lee's knowledge of drumming came not from music school but from his three percussionist brothers at home; from lessons at high school; and, perhaps most importantly, from his peers.

> Mickey Conway, John Boudreaux and me used to get in Mickey's house and set up three drumsets. He had a good mother and father, they never complained. We'd do this during the summer when school was out, from about twelve o'clock in the day to about six, eight o'clock in the evening. Just trading fills, trading eighths, playing sixteenths, whatever. You know, play up, play slow, play ballads, trading ideas, getting ideas from each other.

Lee followed the music scene closely and was well aware of one of its leading players, Ed Blackwell. "Blackwell was the top jazz drummer in the city," he says, "and everybody wanted to hear him." While in high school, Lee encountered another drummer who would later influence a whole generation of New Orleans musicians: James Black.

> I knew James when I was in ninth grade at Joseph Bescoll High School, studying with Miss Yvonne Bush. James Black was a trumpet player in the concert band and I was a snare drummer under Herbert Taylor. I don't know whether James was playing first, second or third trumpet, but he was playing trumpet in the concert band, to show you what kind of musical understanding this guy had. He was a hell of a musician, man. But I didn't know him that well, I talked to him every now and then. He was playing [drums] with Ellis Marsalis and Nat Perrilliat, and I think I went to hear them once or twice. I was just learning how to play jazz then and they were already playing jazz.

Even as a teenager, Lee took his drumming, and his talent, seriously. Drummer Ernie Elly, who went to the same high school as Lee, remembers, "He had been at it [drumming] a little longer than I had, and I'd just be sittin' back there in amazement. He'd have maybe a telephone book on his drumhead and [would be] going over the rudiments, and I'd sit there with my eyes bulging out and listening, you know."[1] By the time he was in his late teens, Lee was working with R&B artist Eddie Bo, with whom he cut a few sides, including a tune called "The Get Back," which featured some of his funky tom-tom work.

After graduation, Lee joined the 4th Army Band in Texas and later played in the 8th Army Band in Korea. He played mostly snare drum, switching to bass drum on special occasions. The Army band gave Lee an appreciation for a different type of march than was common in New Orleans:

> In the Army Band everybody was in tune, everybody played the tempo, and everybody played what was written. And man, I didn't know a march could be so beautiful, with all these different sounds coming out. You could hear the tubas, trombones, and the drums just comping along in the middle.

When his stint in the Army ended in the mid-sixties, Lee returned to New Orleans and joined Willie Tee and the Souls, which included Earl Turbinton (sax), Wilson Turbinton, aka Willie Tee (keyboards), and George Davis or George French (bass). This experience proved to be a watershed for Lee, who saw the group as the perfect vehicle for his musical ideas.

It just so happened, after high school David Lee went into the army, and I went into the Air Force band. He was in the army band, and I was in an Air Force band, and both of us wound up being stationed in San Antonio. I was at Lockland Air Force Base, and he was at Fort Sam Houston, so I went into a night club one night, and I looked at the drummer, and said, "That looks like David Lee." It was kind of dark, and I said, "You look like David Lee," and he said, "I am David Lee." So we wound up playing different gigs with different cats around that city, and even after that he got stationed, shipped over to Korea, and eventually I got out of the Air Force. When I got out of the Air Force, that's when I went to Grambling. I was in the band, majoring in music there. I left there, and then from there I went to hit the road with Ray Charles, and it seemed that everywhere we went, we would run into one another. One time, at the Fillmore East, I was with Ray Charles and David Lee was with Dizz. So they had two New Orleans drummers with four bands, you know? It seemed like even if we wouldn't meet each other on different gigs, we'd see each other in different joints and all, and he's a beautiful cat. He's a great cat."

—Ernie Elly

I was fortunate enough to play with musicians who wanted to play. Earl Turbinton wanted to play and Willie Tee wanted to play, George Davis wanted to play, George French wanted to play. So when we got together there wasn't no bullshit, you know, we were seriously playing. We would say, "Man, you heard what he did? We could do that!" "No, I don't want to do it like that!" We'd be listening to records, come pick each other up and go to the house and sit down, "Man, I got a new record by Miles," or Coltrane, you know, put it on and listen to what they did.

Willie Tee and the Souls played R&B dates, and formed their own outlet for experiments in jazz, the New Orleans Jazz Workshop. Drummer Johnny Vidacovich, who was greatly influenced by David Lee, remembers the scene:

I used to go to this place called the New World Theater on Decatur Street where Willie Tee, Earl Turbinton, George Davis and David Lee used to play. Since it was not a bar, you didn't have to be a certain age to get in. I used to go there at least five nights a week and I used to take my college homework and work on it before or while they played. They would wait until enough people came in, maybe 15 or so people, and then they would play until they felt like not playing. It was one of those places, a couple of cokes, couple of dollars, and you were in. I think the musicians were paid from the local arts council or something. That's where I used to go to check out David.

David was always taking a chance, moving forward, even at the risk of being criticized or not sounding good, but at least he was trying something new, extending, extending, extending. He wasn't trying new stuff to be freaky, he would take stuff that was very conventional and freak it just a little bit to see the possibilities that might come as a result. That's one thing I really love about him. I got my ideas about playing time, and not playing time, from listening to him over and over again. He would do things that were very timely, then he would lay out and come back in playing an unconventional pattern, and all of this would be going on while they were playing a tune. So I began to put two and two together and I realized that there are just a few things you do and what makes it happen is where you do them. But whatever you do, have some sort of logic to it. Make things symmetrical. You can do anything freaky if you make it symmetrical—then it's not so freaky.[2]

Lee himself recalls how the band developed its music:

I used to play timpani and other percussion instruments in the concert band, and so when I listened to music I would hear [that] the drums shouldn't be playing in this spot, or this should be a timpani roll in here, and I started to play like that. And Willy and [the others] went with me to the point where we didn't sound like nobody around here.

One night in 1969, as Lee was playing the Horse Stable on Bourbon Street with bassist George French's Funk Incorporated, Dizzy Gillespie stopped by.

Dizzy came in, introduced himself and told me his drummer had just given him two weeks' notice. He said he liked the way I played and would I join his band? I told him no, because I was making $350 a week on Bourbon Street and he's talking about $300 a week to go fly off to somewhere I don't know nothin' about!

Gillespie returned the following night, however, and Lee reconsidered.

I told him, "Well, look, if you can get me some drums," because my drums were pretty shabby, "and some cymbals and stuff, I'll take a chance and go out with you."

Lee stayed with Gillespie for about a year, appearing on his release entitled *The Real Thing* (Perception Records). At the time, boogaloo was the beat everyone was playing and raving about, as popularized by groups like Sly and the Family Stone. Gillespie also experimented with the new rhythm. "Dizzy was bridging the gap between boogaloo, swing and be-bop," Lee says. "At the same time, Miles decided to go all the way: Miles went with funk and electric pianos and all that stuff, but Dizzy was still tampering around with the boogaloo and still playing straight-ahead bebop." Lee's boogaloo beats had a jazz ride feel on the cymbal and a New Orleans second line feel between the snare and bass drums, freeing the bass player to walk or break up the rhythm. The result was similar to today's hip-hop grooves; in fact, Lee says, "They call it hip-hop today, but it was called boogaloo in the sixties."

After he left Gillespie's band Lee moved to New York, where his career began to take off. He lent his talents, along with drummers Billy Cobham and Billy Hart, to Joe Zawinul's pre-Weather Report recording *Zawinul*. He also recorded and toured with Roy Ayers and Lonnie Liston Smith, and in

1972 joined Sonny Rollins's band. Lee stayed with Rollins until 1975 and appeared on three recordings, *Next Album, Horn Culture,* and *The Cutting Edge.* These three albums accurately document Lee's style, with his clear, explosive cymbal work, interesting interplay and comping, and constantly shifting, organic grooves. The looseness evident on these recordings—still fresh-sounding after 20 years—comes, Lee says, from the freedom given the musicians by the bandleader.

> *People listen to the things I played with Sonny Rollins or Dizzy Gillespie and they think, "Oh, Dizzy [or Sonny] must have told him to play that." They didn't. They just said, "This is eight bars and then we make a break and you figure out what rhythm you wanna play." Vernel Fournier, when he played that rhythm on "Poinciana," he made a hit for Ahmad Jamal, but Ahmad Jamal didn't tell him to play like that. I couldn't see Ahmad Jamal comprehending how to do the drums like that.*

Lee spent most of the seventies in New York and was very active on the jazz scene, recording and performing with Chet Baker, Frank Weiss, Albert Daily, Charlie Rouse, Gary Burton, Larry Coryell and many others, and giving clinics and lectures at Jazz Interactions in New York City and the University of Connecticut. In 1975 Lee formed his own quintet. The group's one album, *Evolution* (out of print), featured David's compositions, including a suite for drums that showed the combined influence of Baby Dodds, Max Roach and Lee's own New Orleans roots.

Due in part to poor health, Lee reluctantly left New York and returned to New Orleans in the late seventies. Although his playing has been sporadic since then, he has performed with Ellis Marsalis (whose album *Ellis Marsalis A Night at Snug Harbor, New Orleans* is a swinging record and a superb document of Lee's playing) and other local jazz greats and has recorded with his longtime cohort Earl Turbinton *(Brothers for Life* and *Black Leaves),* as well as contributing to several R&B albums on Blacktop Records. Lee continues to teach and remains actively interested in the jazz scene, both in New Orleans and elsewhere.

SOURCES
The Encyclopedia of Jazz in the 70s, Leonard Feather & Ira Gitler

QUOTES
All David Lee quotes are from an interview with Dan Thress New Orleans, April, 1994
1 Ernie Elly interview with Dan Thress, New Orleans, May 1994.
2 Johnny Vidacovich interview with Dan Thress, New Orleans, May 1994.

DAVID LEE SELECTED DISCOGRAPHY

Roy Ayers *He's Comin';* **Chet Baker** *My Funny Valentine* (Philology), *Live In Paris, 1960–3 & Nice, 1975* (FDC 123); **Gary Burton–Larry Coryell** (Atlantic); **Dizzy Gillespie** *The Real Thing* (Perception); **David Lee, Jr.** *Evolution* (SES, out of print); **Ellis Marsalis** *Live At Snug Harbor, New Orleans* (somethin'else/Evidence); **Sonny Rollins** *Next Album, Horn Culture, The Cutting Edge* (Original Jazz Classics); **Charlie Rouse** *Two Is One* (Strada East); **Lonnie Liston Smith** (Polydor); **Earl Turbinton** *Black Leaves, Brothers For Life* (with Willie Tee); **Richard Wyands** *Then, Here And Now* (Storyville); **Thunderbird Davis** *Checkout Time* (Black Top); **Grady Gaines** *Full Gain* (Black Top); **Teddy Renoldys** *Gulf Coast Blues* (Black Top); **Joe Zawinul** *Zawinul* (Atlantic/Rhino).

When I learn a pattern, or when I take a pattern that I like and try to adapt it to music, I'll sit down and see how I can fit that pattern into a tune. The way I do that is to take a simple tune and practice a very simple rhythm, and then try to go into another sort of second line street beat type of feel. So let's take "You Are My Sunshine," and I'll play it very straight for the first time through, and then the second time through I'll play a little street type of beat, and the third time through, I'll try to play a reggae type of beat.

If you're thinking too much about the pattern you're playing, it takes away from the smoothness and the dance of it. So by singing the melody to a song, you're creating another thing to concentrate on. This way, you have to have your hands and your feet doing the beat automatically while keeping the context and the time of the tune happening, and then switch from beat to beat. Let me try to demonstrate: three times through, three different beats.

Reggae

"NEW DAY"

Your composition "New Day" has kind of a tango feel to it.

Well, I don't know if it is a tango but it sounds like a tango to me and I like to play that kind of beat. As far as the tune goes, though, it's just a 32-bar tune. It really can be played with any type of a feel.

As a matter of fact, when we play that tune, I often shift from the tango feel to a sort of rock quarter-note feel, and then usually double-time it into a jazz feel. So let me play a little bit of it and you can hear how it all relates. The drums start out with a tango feel, and then as we improvise it gets a little funkier, and then eventually we go to swing and then come back down just like we went up.

CD TRACK 65

This interesting recording showcases Johnny in a trio setting, with saxophonist Tony Dagradi and bassist James Singleton. Johnny approaches the trio like a piano player or a guitarist, always outlining the form, and providing superb accompaniment. Lots of feel changes.

Turnipseed Music TMCD.07

"New Day"

DRUMS

Form: AABA
Solos: Sax 1 chorus
  Piano 1 chorus (double-time swing)
  Drums 1 chorus

"New Day" Drum Solo

Here is a transcription of Johnny's solo on "New Day." The length of the solo is one chorus. Johnny takes a melodic approach to this solo, using mallets, and playing phrases that anticipate and shade the harmonic motion of the piece.

sticks

Back to head

"BONGO JOE"

What about the tune "Bongo Joe?" That shifts between two interesting grooves.

Well, it's a crazy song. When James (Singleton) brought that tune in, I heard it as two different sections with a little turn-around trip at the end of the second section. The first part is in one tonality, and the second part in another. I'm going to take a chance and label it, but as I said, my labels are not very accurate—I approach it like a zydeco beat on the first part of the tune, or like a cajun beat. Let me just play a little bit of a cajun beat.

Or even simpler, it would be: (plays)

Now what I do is I just kind of jazz it up, play it on the snare drum, add some ruffs and drags, and "street" beats moving around the different parts of the drum for different sounds. I came up with this kind of beat:

Cajun people usually dance at about that tempo and they usually stay with that sort of beat. Now, in the second part of the tune, I stay away from the downbeat and try to make sort of a reggae groove out of it, which is like this:

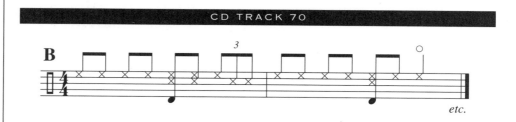

So now with the two beats together. If I make a smooth enough transition, the tune sounds like it has two balanced halves, because the first half of the tune with the zydeco beat is very downbeat-oriented, and it also has a *boom-tacka-boom-tacka-boom-tacka*—and the reggae groove that I switch to is half that tempo, and the backbeat is on the other part—creating an entirely different emphasis. So let's see what it sounds like when we mix them together.

So I just try to mix the two beats together.

They do complement one another.

Yeah, I just—I experimented a few times at rehearsals—and on the gig—to rely on those two beats to get me through the tune.

"Bongo Joe"

CD TRACK 71

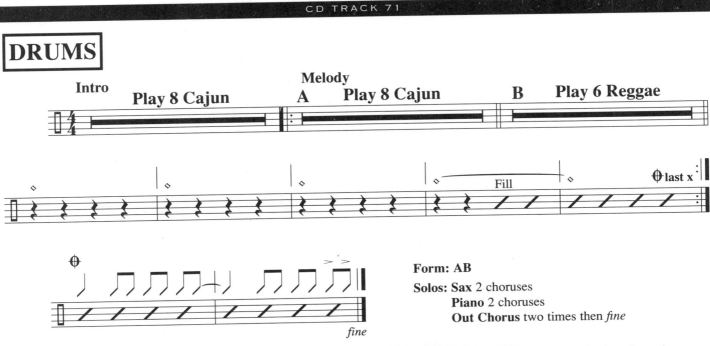

Form: AB

Solos: **Sax** 2 choruses
Piano 2 choruses
Out Chorus two times then *fine*

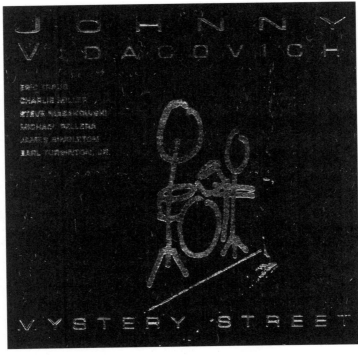

DR Music

This solo release from Johnny features several great musicians, including saxophonist Eric Traub and guitarist Steve Masakowski. A musically diverse recording.

JOHNNY VIDACOVICH by Dan Thress

Wide Open

WWOZ Jazz Tent, New Orleans Jazz and Heritage Festival, April 30, 1993

It never stopped raining the whole second week of Jazz Fest '93, and though all eleven stages at the Fair Grounds Race Track were covered to keep the performers dry, only a couple offered shelter for the fans. Fortunately, one of them was the WWOZ Jazz Tent. Stepping carefully on straw thrown over the encroaching mud, we entered a tent packed full of enlightened locals, enthusiastic out-of-towners and folks just trying to stay dry, to hear some divinely inspired music. At its center, drawing us all in, was an unmistakable presence: drummer Johnny Vidacovich, who grooved, amused and propelled his captivating band, led by guitarist Steve Masakowski.

My first impression of Vidacovich was how he constantly shapes and moves the music, always in control but never dominating. As with all great jazz, funk and latin players, Vidacovich recognizes how absolutely hip the quarter-note can be: from the first downbeat the band was hittin' it hard, driven by his relentless cymbal and cross-stick quarter-note, funky, "world beat" groove. In their version of Wes Montgomery's "Four and Six," John created an intimate, swingin' atmosphere in an open-air tent in the middle of the day. On Masakowski's tune "Stepping Stone," a funky latin 8th-note feel, Vidacovich laid down two and four with the cross-stick to create another one-of-a-kind beat, strong and enticing to

solo over. I've always dug jazz players who aren't afraid to play backbeats. John is like that: he defines time with his cymbals while his bass drum blends with the upright bass. In the middle of "Stepping Stone," he suddenly got up and walked offstage, leaving saxophonist Tony Dagradi to play trio with pianist Michael Pellera and bassist James Singleton. A few minutes later, he sneaked back into the song with a half-time reggae feel that somehow evolves into a 6/8 groove and then to a double-time swing—all effortless-sounding. The effect on the listener is a sense of change and progression: Dagradi starts to burn and John opens it up even further, til the feel is wide open and sounds like it could go in any direction at any moment.

On "Southern Blue," a moody, Mingus-esque piece, the fat brushes John started with soon turned into sticks that laid down some good southern quarter-notes on his ride cymbal. Dagradi's energetic "Nose Dive" followed, played with a kind of "rock and bop" feel. John took the second solo and stated the melody on drums to cue his bandmates back in. "Hector's Lecture," written for percussionist Hector Gallardo, was the wrap-up, with Hector laying down the clave rhythm, John driving it with quarter-notes, and Masakowski and Dagradi trading solos,

New Orleans Jazz and Heritage Festival, 1993

opening finally onto Gallardo's timbale solo, which John accompanied with hi-hat and small tom before kicking it back into the romping head of the tune.

And that's it—the set ended, and before the applause had stopped, Vidacovich had strapped his backpack on and was heading with Singleton across the muddy grass to the Lagniappe tent to play the 3:00 show with vocalist Betty Shirley.

Saxophonist Eric Traub and pianist Larry Seiberth waited as Vidacovich and Singleton attached cymbals to stands and uncovered the bass; then, without delay, all launched straight into the first number, "Bye Bye Blackbird." John was messing around from the get-go, playing the head as a light samba that propelled the tune into double-time swing, then to a latin feel for the first half of the piano solo. It became obvious that all these tunes could go in almost any direction rhythmically; Vidacovich and bassist Singleton complemented each other perfectly, making the changes sound easy and natural.

The second tune, a two-handed shuffle that let Shirley do her thing, found John mixing it up during the tenor solo, varying the strength of the backbeat. I was struck by how comfortable John is playing the drums—sort of like a pitcher who is trying to get out in front of the hitter: instead of overpowering him, he torments him with curve balls, knucklers and change-ups. Next came a second line version of "Caravan," with John playing the melody on the drums. The crowd clapped along to John's backbeats on the last song, the traditional "Down by the Riverside," creating a spirited revival-meeting mood. And though the tune seemed like the perfect ending to an intense and entertaining afternoon of music, you knew that in five minutes another group and then another and another would take the stage. The crowds of people moved from R&B, gospel and traditional jazz to cajun, Afro-Caribbean or what-have-you, and the rain continued to fall, only adding to the adventure.

James Singleton, Johnny Vidacovich, Tony Dagradi

JOHNNY VIDACOVICH SELECTED DISCOGRAPHY

Johnny Adams *Good Morning Heartache, The Real Me, Walking On A Tightrope* (Rounder); **Mose Allison** *My Backyard* (Blue Note); **Ray Anderson** *Blues Bred In The Bone* (Enja); **Tony Dagradi** *Live at the Columns* (Turnipseed), *Dreams Of Love* (Rounder), *Lunar Eclipse* (Gramavision), *Images From The Floating World* (Core); **Professor Longhair** *Crawfish Fiesta* (Alligator Records); **Steve Masakowski** *What It Was* (Blue Note), *Mars* (Nebula); **Charles Neville and Diversity** (LaserLight); **Charlie Rich** *Pictures and Paintings* (Sire); **Alvin "Red" Tyler** *Graciously, Heritage* (Rounder); **John Scofield** *Flat Out* (Gramavision); **Roland Stone** *Remember Me*; **David Torkanowsky** *Steppin' Out* (Rounder), **Johnny Vidacovich** *Mystery Street*

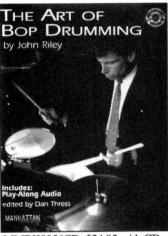

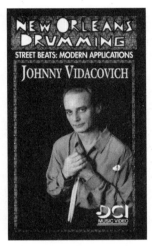

Funeral for Freddie Kohlman

"But to me, the drums are it. And I like the drums to do it, play some down-to-earth, funky swing. In the gutter, on the sidewalk—you know, anywhere you want to. I can appreciate some ways of playing but that's what they're supposed to be about."

—James Black
Melody Maker
August 11, 1973